SILVER BAY PUBLIC LIBRARY
Silver Bay, Minn. 55614

W9-BCW-330

WITHDRAWN

05/8
09/11

783.6
E

Ehret

   The International book of Christmas
carols

SILVER BAY PUBLIC LIBRARY
SILVER BAY, MINNESOTA 55614

DEMCO

THE INTERNATIONAL BOOK OF

musical arrangements by   translations and notes by
WALTER EHRET * GEORGE K. EVANS

illustrations by **DON MARTINETTI**
foreword by **NORMAN LUBOFF**

CHRISTMAS CAROLS

THE STEPHEN GREENE PRESS
BRATTLEBORO, VERMONT

Exclusive Distributors to the music trade:
WALTON MUSIC CORPORATION
CHAPEL HILL, NORTH CAROLINA

SILVER BAY PUBLIC LIBRARY
Silver Bay, Minn. 55614

STEPHEN GREENE PRESS EDITION PUBLISHED AUGUST 1980
Second printing October 1980
Third printing July 1981
Fourth printing September 1982

The International Book of Christmas Carols

Originally published in 1963 by Prentice-Hall, Inc.

Copyright © 1963, 1980 by Walter Ehret and
George K. Evans

All rights reserved. No part of this book may be reproduced without written permission from the publisher, except by a reviewer who may quote brief passages or reproduce illustrations in a review; nor may any part of this book be reproduced, stored in a retrieval system, or transmitted in any form or by any means electronic, mechanical, photocopying, recording, or other, without written permission from the publisher.

This book has been produced in the United States of America. It is published by THE STEPHEN GREENE PRESS, Fessenden Road, Brattleboro, Vermont, 05301.

Exclusive distributors to the music trade: WALTON MUSIC CORPORATION, P.O. Box 470, Chapel Hill, NC 27514

Rights for octavo editions are controlled by WALTON MUSIC CORPORATION (A.S.C.A.P.), One Lincoln Plaza, New York, New York, 10023.

COVER ILLUSTRATION: Detail from *Notre Dame de la Belle Verriere,* eleventh-century window in Chartres Cathedral.

Library of Congress Cataloging in Publication Data

EHRET, WALTER, arr.
  The international book of Christmas carols.

  In part for voice and piano; in part for chorus (SATB); words in English or in the original languages with English translations.
  Includes chord symbols for chord organs, accordions, guitars, ukeleles, and other fretted instruments.
  "This book . . . offers 164 carols from all sections of the Western world."
  Reprint of the 1963 ed. published by Prentice-Hall, Englewood Cliffs, N.J.
  1. Carols.   2. Christmas music.   I. Title.
[M2065.E416 1980]   783.6'552   80–13105
ISBN 0–8289–0378–6 (pbk.)

783.6
E

I am not usually given to superlatives but, in this instance, I can't avoid them. In my opinion, *The International Book of Christmas Carols* is a great book.

Much care has gone into the preparation of this book. Lovely and unusually poetic lyric settings are the rule. The inclusion of the texts in their original languages points up how well the new texts have captured the mood and message of the old. Musically, the settings are simple and, though easy to play, are completely satisfying. The arranger has shown unusual restraint and good taste in his ability to make the arrangements colorful without becoming arbitrarily "fancy."

This is a most complete collection of international carols. All the best-known carols, many in their traditional settings, are included. In addition, there are a great many which have not previously appeared in any collection. The Slavic, Scandinavian, and Spanish carols are particularly noteworthy in this respect.

This book is a real contribution, not only to the literature of Christmas music, but to folk music as well.

Norman Luboff

PREFACE

CHRISTMAS is a festival of the heart. Transcending national boundaries and racial distinctions, it speaks from the heart of one individual to another. Nevertheless, it must rely on language for communication, and we have tended to restrict ourselves to celebrating it in our own tongue.

In our shrinking world, language barriers are falling all around us. Our schools, even down to the beginning primary grades, are giving children conversational experience in several languages. Foreign language study is increasing tremendously throughout our educational institutions. We are beginning to realize that the peoples of the world must understand one another if they are to live together, and that a major key to such understanding is being able to converse in each others' native tongues.

What better embodies the hopes of the world than the Christmas prophecy of peace on earth and good will toward men? And what better ground for shared happiness among nations can we find than that offered by the message of the Christmas season? Then why not "tell it on the mountain" in as many lands and tongues as possible?

Questions such as these, and the quickened interest in languages around the world prompted the writing of this book. We felt that it was time to present a liberal cross-section of Christmas songs from many countries *in their original languages,* along with translations that adhere closely to the meaning of the original texts in order to preserve their true flavor.

We have worked to make the book both flexible and useful. The piano accompaniments have been kept simple, but much effort has gone into making them musically interesting and satisfying. Chord indications are given for every carol so that the accompaniments may be played on chord organs, accordions, guitars, ukuleles, and other fretted instruments. A detailed chart demonstrating how to finger chords for fretted instruments is given in the back of the book.

We have been careful to keep the voice ranges of the songs comfortable and the texts singable. Since harmony parts always add much pleasure to singing, we have retained traditional four-part arrangements of the most familiar carols and hymns. For the others, we have provided a second part to go along with the melody (printed in smaller notes) that may be sung, or played on the recorder, flute, violin, or on other non-transposing instruments.

Although we have included many charming and original folk carols, we have not slighted deeply sacred and worshipful hymns. We have striven to choose selections that reflect the gamut of moods and meanings of Christmas.

To give perspective, we begin the book with a résumé of the development of Christmas customs and music. Historical notes on the individual songs and indexes of English and original language titles close it.

Two other people have contributed greatly to this volume: George Chien, who designed the book so beautifully, and Don Martinetti, who provided extraordinarily fine illustrations. We extend our heartfelt gratitude to both.

Welcome to *The International Book of Christmas Carols*! We hope it will make your Christmas more holy, happy, and enriched with new appreciation of our world neighbors.

Walter Ehret
George K. Evans

TABLE OF CONTENTS

GERMAN CAROLS 135

SCANDINAVIAN CAROLS 185

chRistmas anb its songs

HE EARLIEST SOURCE of Christmas customs is probably the Sumerian civilization which flourished over 4000 years ago.

Marduk, the chief god of Sumer, won that position by engaging in a titanic battle with Tiamat, the goddess monster who ruled the underworld kingdom of Chaos. Marduk killed her and fashioned the world from her corpse.

This world of Marduk's making had to be rejuvenated periodically. When vegetation withered and died, and leaves fell from the trees, the world was running down. Chaos was closing in to take revenge for Tiamat's death.

An elaborate festival, *Zagmuk,* was established to persuade Marduk to return to the underworld and battle Chaos for another cycle of seasons. *Zagmuk* lasted for twelve days and began with the people purifying themselves from the sins of the past year by transferring all sins to the Sumerian king, who was to die for their atonement. After his death, the king was to accompany Marduk and fight by his side for the new year. The king, however, did some transferring of his own. He selected a criminal and dressed him in regalia. Then, to make sure that Marduk would be convinced that the substitute was an authentic king, the populace worshiped him ostentatiously for several days. After his short reign, the substitute king was stripped of his regal clothes and slain.

A time of great anxiety and constant prayer followed the substitute king's death, because Marduk was locked in a mortal struggle with the demons of Chaos. Gradually, he gained the advantage. With the turn in the battle, the Sumerians abandoned themselves to celebration: Mock battles dramatized the underworld fight; bonfires blazed and wooden effigies of Tiamat were tossed into them; processions of masqueraders danced and rioted through the streets; good wishes for the new-gained year passed from friend to friend; gifts were exchanged; and everywhere, shouts of thanksgiving and praise rose to Marduk, the deliverer.

Persians and Babylonians followed the traditions of *Zagmuk* set up by the Sumerians, adding a few new touches. In one of their innovations, masters and slaves traded places during the festival, introducing much clowning and horseplay.

As the Mesopotamian civilization grew older, Marduk's character changed. He increasingly controlled the fate of men and ordained their destiny. Magic incantations for health and prosperity joined *Zagmuk,* and the people built their plans for the coming year around fortune predictions. Our New Year's resolutions likely stem from this precedent.

The chief influence of Mesopotamian religion upon Greece and Egypt was through a sun-worshiping cult developed by the Persian prophet, Mithras. Rome also reserved a prominent place for sun worship. According to the Roman Calendar, December 25 was the day the sun reached its weakest point and began to regain its strength. It was also the birthday of Mithras. Romans observed a special ritual on December 25, the *Sol Invictus,* for the sun's replenishment. Candles, representing the sun's returning power, were the symbol of the day. Thousands of them lighted houses, blinked in processions, made temples and entire cities glow.

Greece and Egypt paid scant attention to new year ceremonies. It was Rome that appropriated the traditions of *Zagmuk* in the West, and enlarged upon them.

The Roman god, Saturn, was an agricultural deity. During his festival, *Saturnalia* (December 17 to 24), slaves lorded it over their masters, masquerading and street processions abounded, and good luck charms were favorite gifts. Obviously, these customs had crossed the Mediterranean from Mesopotamia to find a new home.

Unlike the Mesopotamians, the Romans made no attempt to fight the threatening monsters of the underworld. They were content to keep them at bay with magic charms used during *Saturnalia*. Since they refused to die in the winter, evergreen trees were a mighty symbol of life and strong protection against anything that would destroy it. *Saturnalia* saw all Roman houses decorated with evergreen boughs. *Strenae,* small cookies or fruit that warded off evil, were universally given and received as part of the celebration.

Saturnalia was much less grim and serious than *Zagmuk*. Since Saturn was god of the harvest, his holiday concentrated upon feasting, giving thanks for earth's fruitfulness, and offering prayers for her continued abundance. After the prescribed religious ceremonies (which became ever shorter and less important), the populace hurried to banquet tables to eat and carouse. Each year the observance grew more boisterous and licentious until its religious significance almost completely disappeared.

Meanwhile, far to the north of Rome, Celtic and Teutonic tribes had developed gods and rituals of their own to assure protection and assistance in the new year. Woden (Odin in Scandinavian countries), a giant fellow who wore a floppy, wide-brimmed hat and rode an incredibly swift, eight-legged horse, was their chief god. Warlike, but very wise, Woden fought against the giants in the earth that were constantly seeking to destroy his people. Later, as we shall see, Woden assumes a specific role in our celebration of Christmas.

Life was hard in the severe northern climate. Plans had to be laid carefully at the onset of the long winter to make certain that there would be enough food to last until spring. If herds were large, they had to be thinned, because they would eat too much precious stored food. Stock-slaughtering and meat-curing time offered an opportunity to invite neighbors in for a feast, to thank the gods for the past year, and to pray for another revolution of the wheel of the seasons.

The menace of the cruelly cold, long nights as well as that of the giants who might rush from the bowels of the earth at any moment and overwhelm the people demanded strong protective measures. In addition to the aid of the gods, the northmen relied heavily on magic symbols and charms. Even more than the Romans, they depended upon evergreens to shield them against their enemies. Holly, pine, bay, spruce, laurel, ivy, fir—the aid of every conceivable bush and tree of lasting green was invoked. Celtic priests, the Druids, attributed miraculous healing powers to mistletoe and included it in their sacred rituals. The light and heat of fire was also considered helpful magic. Bonfires of large logs burned during the new year observance were the forebears of the Yule log of today.

❋   ❋   ❋

In this pagan setting, Christ made his appearance. His birthdate was hardly noted for some time, even by Christians. To them, the Resurrection was the important thing, and they expected him to return any day.

CHRISTMAS AND ITS SONGS

Telesphorus, the second bishop of Rome (129–138) ordained that "in the holy night of the Nativity of our Lord and Savior, they do celebrate public church services, and in them solemnly sing the Angels' Hymn, because also the same night he was declared unto the shepherds by an angel, as the truth itself doth witness." Theophilus, who was Bishop of Caesarea during this same period, urged that "the observance or celebration of the birthday of our Lord [be held] on what day soever the 25 of December shall happen."

There was opposition: Origen, one of the great leaders of the early church, proclaimed in 245 that it was a sin to observe Christ's birthday as if he were an Egyptian Pharaoh. December 25 was not officially designated as Christmas and a church festival until sometime between 325 and 350.

During the sixth century, Dionysius Exiguus, a Roman monk, conducted investigations to determine the year Christ was born. It was Dionysius' idea to divide history into two eras, B.C. and A.D., with Christ's birth date as the separation point. He calculated that the Nativity occurred in the year 754 of the Roman calendar, and our calendar is based on his conclusion. The New Testament offers contradictory evidence in several places, and archaeological findings corroborate its statements. The year 7 B.C. (the Roman year 747) appears to be the actual year of Christ's birth.

As the Christian faith spread, it ran headlong into the various pagan cults. Converted Romans were extremely hard to wean away from their pagan observances. Loath to give up the frivolity and feasting of *Saturnalia,* they were also afraid to ignore the prayers of *Sol Invictus*: What if the sun should become angry and refuse to return? The old gods of Greece were equally difficult to displace. Many converts played it safe and observed the rituals of both the pagan gods and Christianity.

Hateful as pagan bacchanales were to the early church leaders, no matter how hard they battled, they could not eradicate them. The best they could do was to Christianize them. Sun worship was replaced by worship of the Son of Righteousness; magic and sooth-saying gave way to reading of the Scriptures. But down through the centuries, the ribaldry, the buffoonery, and the debauchery of the old pagan rites have lingered. Nowadays, they have been relegated largely to Hallowe'en, New Year's, and Mardi Gras, but they are still with us!

At the same time, the ascetic severity of the first Christians became tempered with human alloys. The faith developed a heart, and flesh and blood. It turned its gaze on both earth and heaven. In the forefront of this humanization was the figure of Christ himself. The stern arbiter of the last judgment was joined by the defender of the woman taken in adultery, and the man who forgave his enemies during his agony on the cross.

As interest in Christ's earthly experiences grew, the circumstances of his birth became a major center of attention. This inevitably led to a particular interest in his mother. Mary had been considered a saint of the church for centuries, but only now did she begin to receive homage as the blessed virgin who was chosen to be the mother of God. Commenting on the virgin birth in his excellent little book, *4000 Years of Christmas,* Earl W. Count says:

> It is a thought which for centuries the minds of ignorant and educated alike have
> striven to comprehend. How they have striven, and how in their utmost they have

yet realized that they have never quite comprehended, is written in the record of the jewel-covered Bambino in the manger which stands in the Italian churches at Christmas time; in the hymns of the Greek and the Latin churches; in the *Ave Maris Stella, the Stabat Mater,* the *Ave Maria;* in the quaint fancies of the carols from Bohemia, Flanders, the Tyrol; the dramatic re-enacting, at Christmastime, both in church and market-place, of the Gospel stories of the Nativity; and the many, many pictures and statues of the Madonna and Child which have come down the years to tell us how mightily a great thought had seized upon the faith of our forebears.

Christ's baptism by John the Baptist, set as occurring on January 6, was equally as significant for the early church as the Nativity. This twelfth day after Christmas had another distinction: It was the day the Wise Men arrived at Bethlehem and presented their gifts. The date, known as Epiphany, is still an important festival of the church. In many countries it climaxes the Christmas season and is the time that gifts are exchanged.

While the festival of Christmas was being developed by the church at Rome, a priest named Nicholas was serving churches in Asia Minor. As a young man, he was consecrated Archbishop of Myra, an important seacoast town. Not much is known of his life, but he was greatly venerated throughout the land and exerted a strong influence on the entire Byzantine branch of Christendom. Soon after his death on December 6, 326, he became known as Saint Nicholas. Officially, he was made patron saint of the Russian Orthodox Church, and unofficially, of all seamen, travelers, and children.

Many legends grew up about Nicholas' generosity and unselfishness. He was particularly the benefactor of poor and humble people. His many gifts were always given secretly, in the dead of night, so that the recipients would never know who gave them.

When the tribes of the north were converted to Christianity, legends of Nicholas mingled with those of Woden, the Teutonic god. The resulting figure became the Saint Nicholas who rides a white horse through central and northern Europe on December 6 and quizzes children to see if they have behaved properly during the past year. Eventually the same personality crossed the Atlantic to become the American Santa Claus.

❅   ❅   ❅

We have briefly reviewed some of the paths by which Christmas found its place in history. But what of the music of Christmas? Where did it come from?

As with most early Christian hymns, the first Christmas hymns were probably sung to the melodies of Jewish temple hymns and psalms.

In addition to the angels' song, *Gloria in Excelsis Deo,* other great hymns of the early church concerned themselves with Christmas, among them *Veni Redemptor* (Come, Redeemer) attributed to Saint Ambrose, and *Corde Natus Ex Parentis* (Of the Father's Love Begotten) by Prudentius. These highly spiritual expressions were used as an integral part of the worship service.

Carols were a very different breed from the hymns. They derived from secular, pagan sources. Greeks had used them in their plays; Romans, in *Saturnalia.* They were a popular part of village festivals, weddings, and birthdays. The word *carol* originally referred to a circle dance which, for a long time, was danced without being sung.

4

When words were added, at first they were likely used merely as an accompaniment to the dance movements.

As the church struggled against the influences of pagan customs, she sternly barred carols from sacred services. But outside the church, Nativity carols appeared in increasing quantities and flourished. Nearly all were simple folk songs that sprang from the hearts of humble country people.

Saint Francis of Assisi is credited with bringing carols into the formal worship of the church. In 1223, Francis was conducting Christmas services at Grecchio, in the province of Umbria. For some time, he had been seeking a way to present the concept of the Incarnation of God to his parish. On Christmas Eve, he borrowed some farm animals, collected the trappings of a stable, and placed a statue of the infant Christ in a manger filled with hay. In a cave near the ancient castle of Grecchio, he arranged them to re-create the setting of the first Christmas night. By special permission of the Pope, Francis was allowed to conduct a midnight Mass before his handiwork. Friars composed and sang new, joyful songs much more akin to carols than hymns to accompany the tableau. Thus, the way was opened for the church and carols to become reconciled. Manger scenes (known as a *crèche* in France, a *presebre* in Italy, and a *nacimiento* in Spain) universally present in the Christmas observances of all Mediterranean countries and Latin America stem from Saint Francis' presentation.

Carols enjoyed further development and popularity through their connection with the mystery plays of the Middle Ages. A complex of pageantry, revelry, piety, and song, the mysteries were dramatizations of biblical stories, usually presented in conjuction with major church festivals.

Among the mysteries, two of the most favored and long-lived were the Donkey's Festival (*Fête de l'Âne*), performed for Christmas, and the Feast of Fools (*Fête de Foux*), performed for New Year's.

The Donkey's Festival, a re-enactment of the Holy Family's flight to Egypt, was performed most colorfully at Beauvais and Sens in France. The donkey carrying Mary was arrayed in all the colors of the rainbow. The huge procession which surrounded and followed the family group as it wound its way through the narrow streets sang a hymn of praise to the donkey set to an old Latin hymn, *Orientis Partibus*. The text ran thus:

> From Eastern lands comes the Donkey,
> Beautiful and strong Donkey,
> Most patient carrier of burdens.
> Hee-haw, Sir Donkey, hee-haw!

The Feast of Fools was a much rowdier, more vulgar procession. Presiding over it was a "Lord of Misrule" or "Abbott of Unreason" (often the village idiot), a direct descendent of the mock king of the early Mesopotamians and leaders of the street processions of *Saturnalia*. His Lordship, mounted on a donkey and dressed as a clown or jester, was attended by a gibbering, capering retinue clad in the most ludicrous attire they could find. Unless forbidden, the procession would move to the cathedral, and proceed down the nave to the altar. There, they would present a parody Mass, including squawking motets by the "choir" and an apish devil's dance.

Carols used with the processional mysteries followed a special pattern. They began with a "burden", or refrain, sung by the spectators as members of the procession danced. A verse sung by a solo voice followed, during which the dancers rested and caught their breath. The burden was repeated, followed by another solo verse, and so on. As might be expected, the carols had many verses, each sandwiched in between the danced burdens. Nearly all were in 3/4 meter, since it lends itself to dancing. Many Spanish carols still retain the burden-verse form.

Not all mystery plays were processions. Some were performed inside the church, and many were presented on a cart divided horizontally into two decks. The lower deck was screened and served as the actors' dressing room. The upper deck formed the stage. A trapdoor was often installed between the decks, which the devil, a great favorite with audiences, used for his entrances and exits. The famous mysteries of Chester and Coventry in England were presented on carts.

A number of the medieval carols have been preserved in manuscript. Their texts are quite intellectual as well as spiritual, indicating they were probably written by clerics. Many others, however, were not written down, but were passed along from generation to generation in the true folk tradition. The topics they treat are seemingly endless. Mystical and fantastic subjects abound, for this was an era when imagination was given full sway. The age which produced the gargoyle and other fanciful creatures surrounded the manger of Bethlehem with talking animals, flocks of worshiping birds, and flowers that bloomed miraculously in the winter night.

French Noëls, among the oldest and most durable of carols, may have derived their name from the Latin word for birthday, Natalis. The first Noëls were supposedly an amalgamation of the songs sung around Saint Francis' manger scene and the songs of troubadours. They form an unbroken line of words and melody that has continued virtually unchanged to the present.

Noëls almost always tell a story, and this same characteristic furnished the name for the early English Ballad Carol, largely developed by wandering minstrels. Dialogues, legends, and lengthy narratives abound in both the Noëls and Ballad Carols.

Our strolling carolers of Christmas are part of a long tradition which extends back through the beggars of the Middle Ages to the exchanged roles of master and slave in pagan festivals. Medieval beggars roamed the streets at Christmastime singing carols to cadge alms or free portions of food and drink. In England, Yule serenaders came to be known as Waits, and they were often rewarded with an invitation to enter the warm house and have a cup of Wassail (hot spiced ale or wine). Only recently has caroling come to be a way of extending charity than of asking it.

The Protestant Reformation resulted in a sharp reduction in secular, boisterous observances of Christmas. The German chorales of Luther and Bach brought the ceremonies back into the church and tied music closely to religious texts. Protestantism asked that Christmas songs avoid secular subjects and remain reverent, which was somewhat of a return to the spirit of the early Christian hymns. Joyful hymns were welcomed, but they should not stray from a scriptural and sacred context. The universal emphasis on congregational singing led to more widespread familiarity with Christmas hymns, and the combining of folk melodies with sacred words that occured in many of them increased their popularity.

The rise of Puritanism brought the greatest opposition to carols, and to the entire tradition of Christmas. The Puritan attitude was set forth by the clergyman Edmund Calamy in a sermon preached in the House of Lords on Christmas Day, 1644:

> This day is commonly called Christmas-day, a day that has heretofore been much abused in superstition and profaneness. It is not easy to say whether the superstition has been the greater, or the profaneness...There is no way to reform it, but by dealing with it as Hezekiah did with the brazen serpent. This year God, by His providence, has buried it in a feast, and I hope it will never rise again.

In 1645, observance of all festival days, including Christmas, was abolished by Cromwell's Parliament. During the twelve years the ban held, the spirit of the carol of the middle ages sickened and died in England. Some hardy specimens survived, such as *The First Nowell* and *The Boar's Head,* but not many.

The United States, closely allied in its early years with Puritanism, spurned most carols, and restricted itself to singing and writing hymns.

In countries not associated with the Reformation or Puritanism, carols continued to be sung, but even there interest in them was waning, and few new ones appeared.

Fortunately, recent years have seen an upsurge of interest in carols. Collections such as the *Oxford Book of Carols* have brought many of them back into favor. English-speaking people are becoming more aware of the rich and varied musical heritage of Christmas from other countries: the dance carols of Scandinavia, the shepherd carols of the Slavic countries, the German lullaby carols, the *posadas* and *villancicos* of Spanish lands, and other gems that form a constantly expanding treasure-trove. They return to add to the joy and brightness of Christmas, making it glow again with the imagination and fantasy that welled from the hearts of simple folk offering their adoration and love to the Babe of Bethlehem.

REFERENCES

Aldington, R., and D. Ames, trans., *Larousse Encyclopedia of Mythology.* New York: Prometheus Press, 1960.

Bramley, H. B., and John Stainer, *Christmas Carols New and Old.* London: Novello, Ewer and Company, ca. 1877.

Count, Earl W., *4000 Years of Christmas.* New York: Henry Schuman, 1948.

Dearmer, P., M. Shaw, and R. Vaughan Williams, eds., *Oxford Book of Carols.* London: Oxford University Press, 1928.

Duncan, E., *The Story of the Carol.* New York: Charles Scribner's Sons, 1911.

Greene, R. L., *The Early English Carol.* Oxford: Clarendon Press, 1935.

Mottinger, Alvina H., *Christmas Carols, Their Authors and Composers.* New York: G. Schirmer, 1948.

Nettel, R., *Carols, 1400–1950.* Bedford: Gordon Frazer, 1956.

Phillips, W. J., *Carols.* London: George Routledge and Sons, 1921.

Routley, Erik, *The English Carol.* London: Herbert Jenkins, 1958.

Sandys, W., *Christmas Carols, Ancient and Modern.* London: R. Beckley, 1833.

Simon, H. W., *A Treasury of Christmas Songs and Carols.* Boston: Houghton Mifflin Company, 1955.

Wasner, Franz, *The Trapp Family Book of Christmas Carols.* New York: Pantheon Books, 1950.

Woodward, G. R., ed., *Piae Cantiones.* London: Plainsong and Medieval Music Society, 1910.

ENGLISH CAROLS

We Wish You a Merry Christmas

Traditional English

Traditional English [WE]

Allegro con brio

We wish you a Mer-ry Christ-mas, We wish you a Mer-ry Christ-mas, We

A NOTE ON THE CHORD DESIGNATIONS USED IN THIS BOOK: Wherever possible, literal indications of chords used in the accompaniments are given. However, in the interest of ease of execution on fretted instruments and chord organs, chord indications for selections with involved harmonic progressions and for those played at rapid tempos have been simplified.

wish you a Mer-ry Christ-mas, And a Hap-py New Year!

Fine

REFRAIN

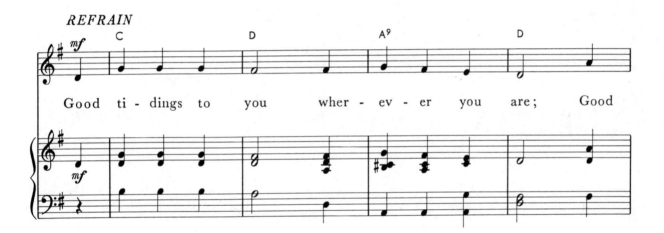

Good ti - dings to you wher - ev - er you are; Good

ti - dings for Christ-mas and a Hap-py New Year! We

D.S.

11

Good Christian Men, Rejoice

John Mason Neale, 1818–1866

14th Century German Carol
Arrangement: John Stainer

1.~3. Good Chris - tian men,___ re - joice___ With

heart, and soul,___ and voice;___

Give ye heed to
Now ye hear of
Now ye need not

what we say: News! News! Je - sus Christ is
end - less bliss: Joy! Joy! Je - sus Christ was
fear the grave: Peace! Peace! Je - sus Christ was

born to-day!   Ox and ass be - fore Him bow, And
born for this!   He hath ope'd the heav'n - ly door, And
born to save!   Calls you one and calls you all, To

He is in ___ the man - ger now;   Christ is born to -
man is bless - ed ev - er - more;   Christ was born for
gain His ev - er - last - ing hall;   Christ was born to

day! _____ Christ is born to - day!
this! _____ Christ was born for this!
save! _____ Christ was born to save!

The Seven Joys of Mary

15th Century English

Traditional English
Arrangement: John Stainer, 1871

Allegretto

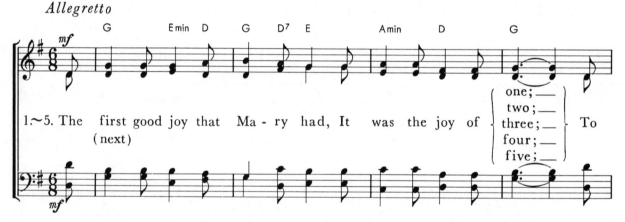

1.~5. The first good joy that Ma - ry had, It was the joy of
(next)

{ one; ___
two; ___
three; ___
four; ___
five; ___ }

To

see the bless - ed Je - sus Christ,
(her own Son)

{ When He was first ___ her son. ___
Mak - ing the lame ___ to go. ___
Mak - ing the blind ___ to see. ___
Read - ing the Bi - ble o'er. ___
Rais - ing the dead ___ to life. ___ }

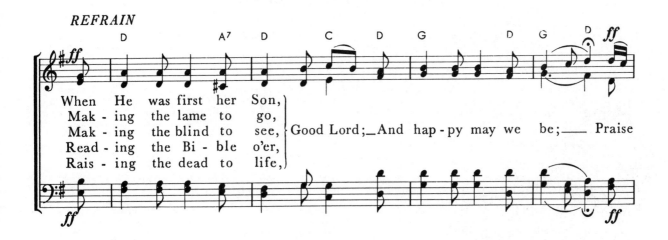

When He was first her Son,
Mak - ing the lame to go,
Mak - ing the blind to see,
Read - ing the Bi - ble o'er,
Rais - ing the dead to life,
Good Lord; And hap - py may we be; Praise

Fa - ther, Son, and Ho - ly Ghost To all e - ter - ni - ty.

6. The next good joy that Mary had,
   It was the joy of six;
   To see her own Son Jesus Christ
   Upon the Crucifix.
   Upon the Crucifix, Good Lord;
   And happy may we be;
   Praise Father, Son, and Holy Ghost
   To all eternity.

7. The next good joy that Mary had,
   It was the joy of seven;
   To see her own Son Jesus Christ
   Ascending into Heaven.
   Ascending into Heaven, Good Lord,
   And happy may we be;
   Praise Father, Son, and Holy Ghost
   To all eternity.

THIS ENDRIS NIGHT

15th Century English

18th Century English Carol [WE]

Andante con moto

1. This en - dris night I saw a sight, A
2. This love - ly la - dy sat and sung, And
3. The Child then spake in His talk - ing, And
4. "For an - gels bright down to me light: Thou

star as bright as day; And e'er a - mong a
to her Child did say: "My son, my broth - er,
to His moth - er said: "Yea, I am known as
know - est 'tis no nay: And for that sight thou

mai - den sung, "Lul - lay, bye bye, lul - lay."
fa - ther, dear, Why liest thou thus in hay?"
hea - ven king, In crib though I be laid."
may'st de - light To sing, 'bye bye lul - lay."

GOOD KING WENCESLAS

John M. Neale, 1853

Piae Cantiones, 1582

1. Good King Wen - ces - las look'd out On the Feast of Ste - phen,
2. "Hith - er, page, and stand by me, If thou know'st it; tell - ing,
3. "Bring me flesh, and bring me wine, Bring me pine - logs hith - er;
4. "Sire, the night is dark - er now, And the wind blows strong - er;
5. In his mas - ter's steps he trod, Where the snow lay dint - ed;

When the snow lay round a - bout, Deep and crisp, and e - ven:
Yon - der peas - ant, who is he? Where and what his dwell - ing?"
Thou and I will see him dine, When we bear them thith - er."
Fails my heart, I know not how, I can go no long - er."
Heat was in the ver - y sod Which the saint had print - ed.

Bright - ly shone the moon that night, Though the frost was cru - el,
"Sire, he lives a good league hence, Un - der - neath the moun - tain;
Page and mon - arch forth they went, Forth they went to - geth - er;
"Mark my foot - steps, my good page, Tread thou in them bold - ly:
There - fore, Chris - tian men, be sure, Wealth or rank pos - sess - ing,

When a poor man came in sight, Gath - 'ring win - ter fu - el.
Right a - gainst the for - est fence, By Saint Ag - nes' foun - tain."
Through the rude wind's wild la - ment, And the bit - ter weath - er.
Thou shalt find the win - ter's rage, Freeze thy blood less cold - ly."
Ye who now will bless the poor, Shall your - selves find bless - ing.

God Rest You Merry, Gentlemen

Traditional 18th Century Carol

Traditional 18th Century London Melody
Harmonization: John Stainer, 1867

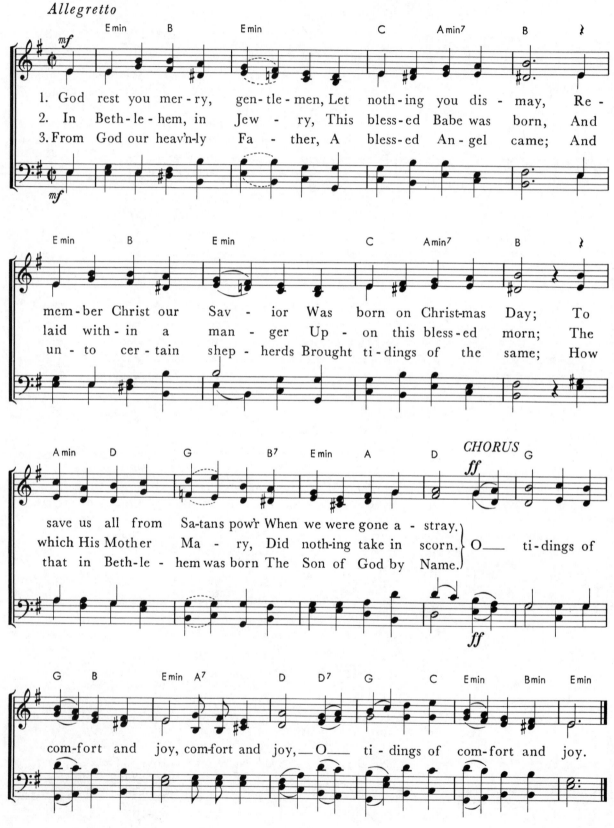

Allegretto

1. God rest you mer-ry, gen-tle-men, Let noth-ing you dis-may, Re-
2. In Beth-le-hem, in Jew-ry, This bless-ed Babe was born, And
3. From God our heav'n-ly Fa-ther, A bless-ed An-gel came; And

mem-ber Christ our Sav-ior Was born on Christ-mas Day; To
laid with-in a man-ger Up-on this bless-ed morn; The
un-to cer-tain shep-herds Brought ti-dings of the same; How

save us all from Sa-tans pow'r When we were gone a-stray.
which His Mother Ma-ry, Did noth-ing take in scorn. O— ti-dings of
that in Beth-le-hem was born The Son of God by Name.

com-fort and joy, com-fort and joy,—O— ti-dings of com-fort and joy.

Coventry Carol

Robert Croo, 1543

English Melody, 1591

Andante sostenuto

1. Lul - lay, Thou lit - tle ti - ny Child, By, by, lul - ly, lul - lay;_____ Lul - lay, Thou lit - tle ti - ny Child, By, by, lul - ly, lul - lay._____
2. O sis - ters, too, how may we do, For to pre - serve this day;_____ This poor Young - ling for whom we sing, By, by, lul - ly, lul - lay._____
3. Her - od the King, in his rag - ing, Charg - ed he hath this day;_____ His men of might, in his own sight, All chil - dren young, to slay._____
4. Then woe is me, poor Child, for Thee, And ev - er mourn and say;_____ For Thy part - ing nor say nor sing, By, by, lul - ly, lul - lay._____

WHEN CHRIST WAS BORN OF MARY FREE

Harleian Manuscript, 1456

16th Century English [WE]

Allegretto moderato

1. When Chist was born of_ Ma - ry_ free, In Beth - le-hem that fair ci - ty,
2. The King is come to_ save man-kind, As in the scrip-ture truths we_ find,
3. Then, dear - est Lord, for_ Thy great_ grace, Grant us in bliss to see Thy_ face,

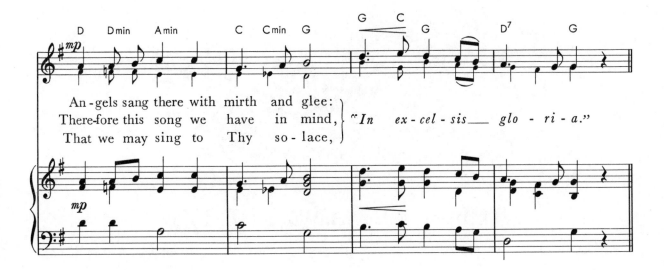

An-gels sang there with mirth and glee:
There-fore this song we have in mind, ⎫ "In ex-cel-sis___ glo-ri-a."
That we may sing to Thy so-lace, ⎭

REFRAIN

In ex-cel-sis glo-ri - a, In ex-cel-sis glo-ri - a,

In ex-cel-sis___ glo-ri - a, In ex-cel-sis glo-ri - a.

In ex-cel-sis___ glo-ri - a, In ex-cel-sis___ glo-ri - a.

THE HOLLY AND THE IVY

Traditional English, ca 1700

Traditional English
Collected and Arranged by
Cecil J. Sharp * [WE]

Allegro

1. The hol-ly and the i - vy, When they are both full grown, Of__
2. The hol-ly bears a blos-som, As white as li - ly flow'r, And__
3. The hol-ly bears a ber - ry, As red as a - ny blood, And__
4. The hol-ly bears a prick - le, As sharp as a - ny thorn, And__
5. The hol-ly bears a bark,__ As bit - ter as the gall, And__
6. The hol-ly and the i - vy, When they are both full grown, Of__

all the trees that are in the wood, The__ hol-ly bears the__ crown:
Ma-ry bore sweet__ Je - sus Christ, To__ be our dear Sav - ior:
Ma-ry bore sweet__ Je - sus Christ, To__ do poor sin - ners__ good:
Ma-ry bore sweet__ Je - sus Christ, On__ Christ-mas day in the morn:
Ma-ry bore sweet__ Je - sus Christ, For__ to re - deem us __ all:
all the trees that are in the wood, The__ hol-ly bears the__ crown:

* By permission of Novello and Co., Ltd.

The ri-sing of the sun___ and the run-ning of the deer, The___

play-ing of the mer-ry or-gan, Sweet sing-ing in the choir.

The Friendly Beasts

Robert Davis*

Medieval French Carol [WE]

1. Je-sus our Broth-er, kind and good, Was hum-bly born in a sta-ble rude, And the friend-ly beasts a-round Him stood.
2. "I," said the cow, all white and red, "I gave him my man-ger for His bed: I gave Him my hay to pil-low His head."
3. "I," said the dove from the raf-ters high, "I cooed Him to sleep so He would not cry, We cooed Him to sleep, my mate and I."

* Copyright 1920 by The H.W. Gray Company (A Division of Belwin-Mills Publishing Corp.).
Copyright renewed 1948. Used by permission.

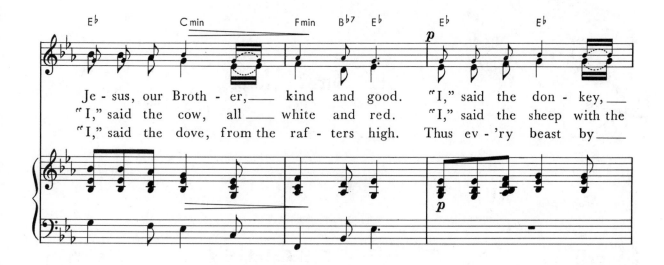

Je - sus, our Broth - er,___ kind and good. "I," said the don - key,___
"I," said the cow, all___ white and red. "I," said the sheep with the
"I," said the dove, from the raf - ters high. Thus ev - 'ry beast by___

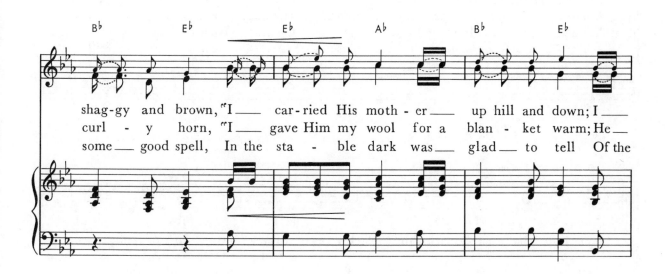

shag - gy and brown, "I___ car - ried His moth - er___ up hill and down; I___
curl - y horn, "I___ gave Him my wool for a blan - ket warm; He___
some___ good spell, In the sta - ble dark was___ glad___ to tell Of the

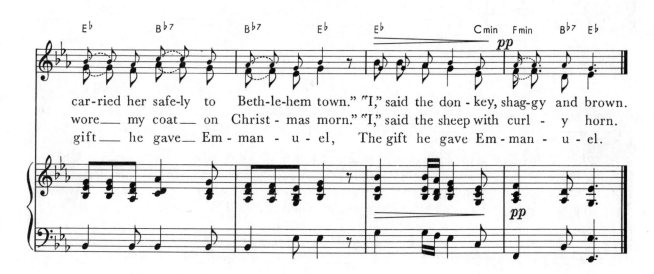

car - ried her safe - ly to Beth - le - hem town." "I," said the don - key, shag - gy and brown.
wore___ my coat___ on Christ - mas morn." "I," said the sheep with curl - y horn.
gift___ he gave___ Em - man - u - el, The gift he gave Em - man - u - el.

25

The First Nowell

Traditional English

Traditional English

Moderato

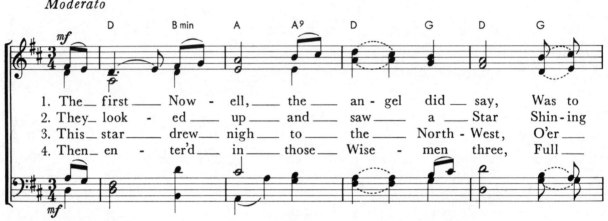

1. The first Now-ell, the an-gel did say, Was to
2. They look-ed up and saw a Star Shin-ing
3. This star drew nigh to the North-West, O'er
4. Then en-ter'd in those Wise-men three, Full

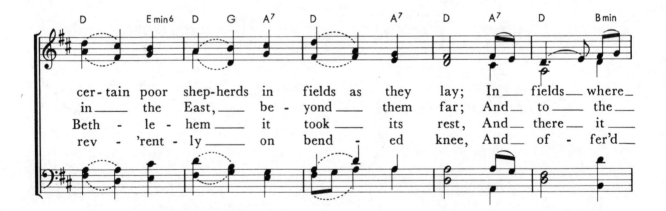

cer-tain poor shep-herds in fields as they lay; In fields where
in the East, be-yond them far; And to the
Beth-le-hem it took its rest, And there it
rev-'rent-ly on bend-ed knee, And of-fer'd

they lay keep-ing their sheep On a cold win-ter's night that
earth it gave great light, And so it con-tin-ued both
did both stop and stay Right o-ver the place where
there in His pres-ence, Their gold and myrrh and

26

REFRAIN

was ___ so deep.
day ___ and night.
Je - sus lay.
frank - in - cense.

Now - ell, ___ Now - ell, Now - ell, ___ Now -

ell, ___ Born is the King ___ of Is - ra - el.

27

JOY TO THE WORLD

Isaac Watts, 1719

Adapted from George F. Handel, 1742

Allegretto

1. Joy to the world! the Lord is come; Let earth re - ceive her
2. Joy to the world! the Sav - ior reigns; Let men their songs em -
3. He rules the world with truth and grace And makes the na - tions

King; Let ev - 'ry heart pre - pare Him room, And
ploy; While field and floods, rocks, hills, and plains Re -
prove The glo - ries of His right - eous - ness, And

28

heav'n and na - ture — sing, And — heav'n and na - ture — sing, And —
peat the sound-ing — joy, Re - peat the sound-ing — joy, Re -
won - ders of His — love, And — won - ders of His — love, And —

And heav'n and na - ture sing, _____
Re - peat the sounding joy, _____
And won - ders of His love, _____

And heav'n and na - ture —
Re - peat the sound-ing —
And won - ders of His —

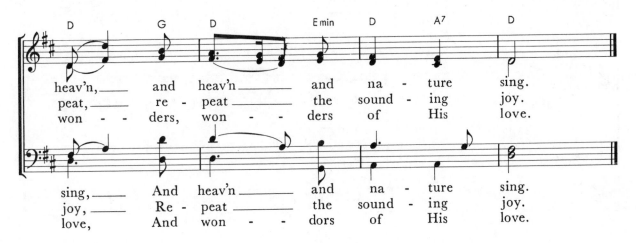

heav'n, _____ and heav'n _____ and na - ture sing.
peat, _____ re - peat _____ the sound - ing joy.
won - ders, won - ders of His love.

sing, _____ And heav'n _____ and na - ture sing.
joy, _____ Re - peat _____ the sound - ing joy.
love, _____ And won - dors of His love.

What Child Is This?

William Dix, ca 1865

17th Century English Air
Arrangement: John Stainer

1. What Child is this, Who, laid to rest On Mary's lap, is sleep-ing? Whom
2. Why lies He in such mean es-tate, Where ox and ass are feed-ing? Good
3. So bring Him in-cense, gold, and myrrh, Come peas-ant, King to own Him, The

an-gels greet with an-thems sweet, While shep-herds watch are keep-ing?
Chris-tian, fear: for sin-ners here The si-lent Word is plead-ing.
King of kings, sal-va-tion brings, Let lov-ing hearts en-throne Him.

REFRAIN

This, this is Christ the King; Whom shep-herds guard and an-gels sing:
Nails, spear, shall pierce Him through, The Cross be borne, for me, for you:
Raise, raise the song on high, The Vir-gin sings her lull-a-by:

Haste, haste to bring Him laud,
Hail, hail, the Word made flesh, The Babe, the Son of Ma-ry!
Joy, joy, for Christ is born,

30

WHILE SHEPHERDS WATCHED THEIR FLOCKS

Nahum Tate, 1652–1715

Arranged from George F. Handel, 1685–1759

Allegro moderato

1. While shep-herds watched their flocks by night, All seat-ed on the ground, The an-gel of the Lord came down, And glo-ry shone a-round, And glo-ry shone a-round.
2. "Fear not!" said he for might-y dread Had seized their trou-bled mind, "Glad tid-ings of great joy I bring, To you and all man-kind, To you and all man-kind.
3. "To you, in Da-vid's town this day, Is born of Da-vid's line, The Sav-ior who is Christ the Lord; And this shall be the sign, And this shall be the sign:
4. "The heaven-ly Babe you there shall find To hu-man view dis-played, All mean-ly wrapped in swath-ing bands, And in a man-ger laid, And in a man-ger laid."

SILVER BAY PUBLIC LIBRARY
Silver Bay, Minn. 55614

Gloucestershire Wassail

Traditional English [alt. GKE]   18th Century Gloucestershire Carol [WE]

1. Was - sail, ___ was - sail ___ all o - ver the town! ___ Our
2. Come, but - ler, and fill us a bowl of your best, ___ And
3. Come here, ___ sweet maid, in the frill - y white smock, ___ Come

bread it is white and our ale ___ it ___ is brown, Our ___
we hope your soul ___ in Heav - en ___ may rest; But ___
trip to the door ___ and trip ___ back ___ the lock! Come ___

32

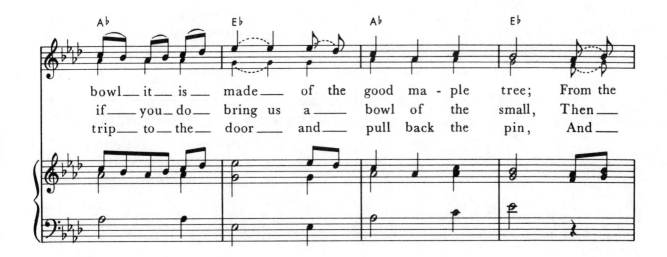

bowl__ it __ is __ made __ of the good ma - ple tree; From the
if __ you __ do bring us a __ bowl of the small, Then __
trip __ to __ the door __ and __ pull back the pin, And __

was - sail - ing bowl __ we'll drink un - to thee.
down shall go __ but - ler and __ bowl __ and all.
let __ us __ jol - ly was - sail - ers in.

The Boar's Head Carol

17th Century English

18th Century English Carol [WE]

Allegro

1. The boar's head in hand bear I, Be-decked with bays and rose-ma-ry; And I
2. The boar's head as I un-der-stand is the fin-est dish in all the land, When
3. Our stew-ard hath pro-vid-ed this In hon-or of the King of Bliss, Which

pray you, my mas-ters, be mer-ry, *Quot es-tis in con-vi-vi-o,*[1]
thus be-decked with a gay gar-land, Let us *ser-vi-re can-ti-co.*[2]
on this day to be serv-ed is, In *Re-gi-nen-si a-tri-o.*[3]

REFRAIN

Ca-put a-pri de-fe-ro, Red-dens lau-des Do-mi-no.[4]

[1]You who are at this feast [2]Serve by singing [3]In the royal hall
[4]The boar's head I bear, Giving praises to the Lord.

Wassail Song

Traditional Yorkshire Carol

19th Century Yorkshire
Arrangement: John Stainer

Allegretto moderato

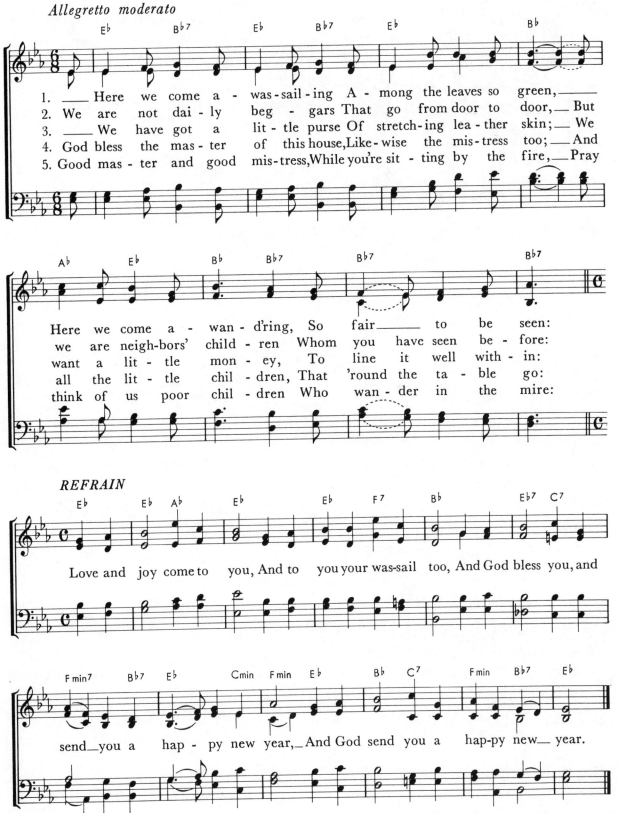

1. ___ Here we come a - was-sail-ing A - mong the leaves so green,___
2. We are not dai - ly beg - gars That go from door to door,__ But
3. ___ We have got a lit - tle purse Of stretch-ing lea - ther skin;__ We
4. God bless the mas - ter of this house, Like-wise the mis-tress too;___ And
5. Good mas - ter and good mis-tress, While you're sit - ting by the fire,__ Pray

Here we come a - wan - d'ring, So fair___ to be seen:
we are neigh-bors' child - ren Whom you have seen be - fore:
want a lit - tle mon - ey, To line it well with - in:
all the lit - tle chil - dren, That 'round the ta - ble go:
think of us poor chil - dren Who wan - der in the mire:

REFRAIN

Love and joy come to you, And to you your was-sail too, And God bless you, and

send_you a hap - py new year,_And God send you a hap-py new_ year.

35

THE TWELVE DAYS OF CHRISTMAS

Traditional English

Traditional English [WE]

Moderato

1. On the first day of Christ-mas my true love sent to me A par-tridge in a pear tree.

2. On the sec-ond
3. On the third____ } day of Christ-mas my true love sent to me.
4. On the fourth____

Two tur-tle doves
Three French hens
Four call-ing birds

And a par-tridge in a pear tree.

D.S. for verses 1–4

D.S. for verses 1–4

(repeat as needed)

5. On the fifth day of Christ-mas my true love sent to me Five gold

rings. Four call - ing birds, Three French hens,

Two— tur-tle doves, And a par-tridge— in a pear tree.

Fine

6. On the sixth—
7. On the sev-enth
8. On the eighth—
9. On the ninth— } day of Christ-mas, my true love sent to me:
10 On the tenth—
11. On the 'le-venth
12. On the twelfth—

C   F   G⁷   C⁷   *to* ✠

for verses 6–12

Six ___ geese a - lay - ing,
Sev - en swans a - swim - ming,
Eight ___ maids a - milk - ing,
Nine ___ la - dies danc - ing,
Ten ___ lords a - leap - ing,
'Le - ven pi - pers pip - ing,
Twelve ___ drum - mers drum - ming,

Five gold ___ rings!

to ✠

for verses 6–12

(repeat as needed)

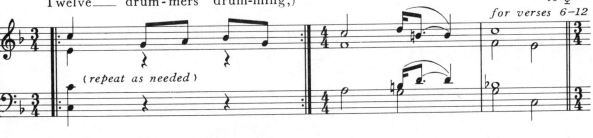

On Christmas Night (Sussex Carol)

Traditional English, alt. [GKE]

Traditional English [WE]

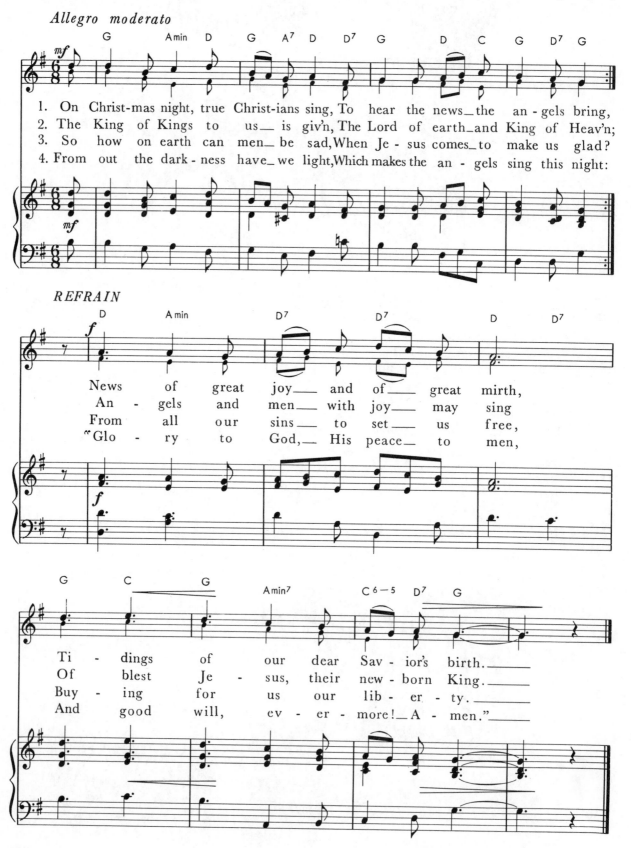

Allegro moderato

1. On Christ-mas night, true Christ-ians sing, To hear the news_the an-gels bring,
2. The King of Kings to us_ is giv'n, The Lord of earth_and King of Heav'n;
3. So how on earth can men_ be sad, When Je-sus comes_to make us glad?
4. From out the dark-ness have_we light, Which makes the an-gels sing this night:

REFRAIN

News of great joy__ and of__ great mirth,
An-gels and men__ with joy__ may sing
From all our sins__ to set__ us free,
"Glo-ry to God,_ His peace_ to men,

Ti-dings of our dear Sav-ior's birth.___
Of blest Je-sus, their new-born King.___
Buy-ing for us our lib-er-ty.___
And good will, ev-er-more!_A-men."___

Blessed Be That Maid Marie

Traditional English

William Ballet's Lute Book [WE]

Andante con moto

1. Bless-ed be that Maid Ma-rie;___ Born__He__was of__ her__ bod-y;
2. Sweet and bliss-ful was the__song___ Chan-ted__ by the__ an-gel__throng,
3. Make we mer-ry on this__fest,___ *In__ quo__Christ-us__ na-tus__ est;*

Ver-y__God ere__ time__be-gan, Born__in__time the__ Son__of__Man.
"Peace__on__earth," Al-le-lu-ya. *In__ ex-cel-sis__ Glo-ri-a.*
On__this__Child I__ pray__you__call, To__ as-soil and__ save__us__ all.

E-ya! Je-sus ho-di-e___ Na-tus__est de__ Vir-gi-ne.

A Virgin Unspotted

Traditional English

18th Century English Carol [WE]

Allegretto

1. A — vir-gin un - spot-ted, the — proph-et fore - told, Should —
2. Then — God sent an — an-gel from — Hea - ven so high, To —
3. Then — pres-ent - ly aft - er, the — shep-herds did spy Vast —
4. To — teach us hu - mil-i - ty — all — this was done, And —

bring forth a — Sav — ior, which — we — now be - hold; To —
cer - tain poor — shep-herds in — fields — where they lie, And —
num - bers of — an - gels to — stand — in the sky; They —
learn we from — thence haugh-ty — pride — for to shun; A —

be our Re - deem - er from death, hell, — and sin, Which —
bade them no long - er in sor - row — to stay, Be -
joy - ful - ly talk - ed and sweet - ly — did sing: "To —
man - ger His cra - dle who came from — a - bove, The —

Ad-am's trans - gres - sion had wrap - ped us in.
cause that our Sav - ior was born on this day.
God be all glo - ry, our heav - en - ly King."
great God of mer - cy, of peace and of love.

REFRAIN

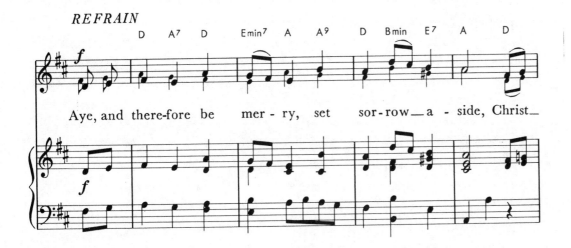

Aye, and there-fore be mer - ry, set sor - row a - side, Christ

Je - sus, our Sav - ior, was born on this tide.

Once in Royal David's City

Cecil F. Alexander, 1848

Henry J. Gauntlett, 1858

Sleep, Holy Babe

Edward Caswall, 1814–1878

John B. Dykes, 1823–1876

Andante moderato

1. Sleep, ho - ly Babe! Up - on Thy mother's breast; Great
2. Sleep, ho - ly Babe! Thine an - gels watch a - round, All
3. Sleep, ho - ly Babe! While I with Ma - ry gaze In

Lord of earth and sea and sky, How sweet it is to see Thee lie In
bend-ing low with fold-ed wings, Be - fore th'in-car-nate King of kings, In
joy up - on that face a - while, Up - on the lov-ing in - fant smile, Which

such a place of rest, In such a place of rest.
rev - 'rent awe pro - found, In rev - 'rent awe pro - found.
there di - vine-ly plays, Which there di - vine-ly plays.

HARK! THE HERALD ANGELS SING

Charles Wesley, 1739
Altered by George Whitfield, 1753

Felix Mendelssohn, 1840
Arrangement: William Cummings, 1850

Andante con moto

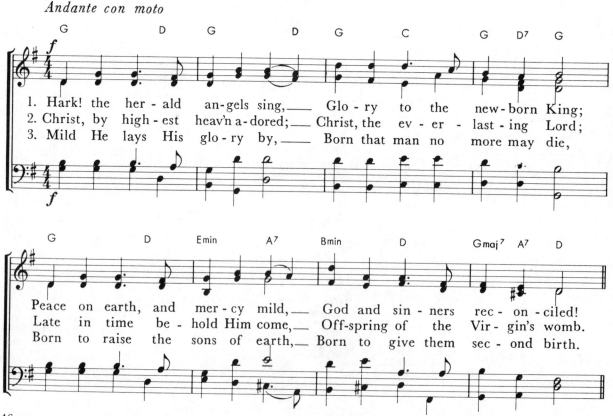

1. Hark! the her-ald an-gels sing,— Glo-ry to the new-born King;
2. Christ, by high-est heav'n a-dored;— Christ, the ev-er-last-ing Lord;
3. Mild He lays His glo-ry by, — Born that man no more may die,

Peace on earth, and mer-cy mild,— God and sin-ners rec-on-ciled!
Late in time be-hold Him come,— Off-spring of the Vir-gin's womb.
Born to raise the sons of earth,— Born to give them sec-ond birth.

Joy-ful all ye na-tions, rise,— Join the tri-umph of the skies;—
Veil'd in flesh the God-head see;— Hail th'In-car-nate De - i - ty,—
Ris'n with heal-ing in His wings,— Light and life to all He brings,—

With th'an-gel-ic host pro-claim, Christ is— born in Beth-le-hem.
Pleased as Man with man to dwell, Je - sus,— our Em-man-u-el!
Hail, the Sun of Right-eous-ness! Hail, the—heav'n born Prince of Peace!

REFRAIN

Hark! the her-ald an-gels sing,— Glo-ry— to the new-born King.

As with Gladness Men of Old

William C. Dix, 1860

Arranged from Conrad Kocher, 1838

Moderato

1. As with gladness men of old Did the guiding star behold;
2. As with joyful steps they sped To that lowly manger bed,
3. As they offered gifts most rare, At that manger rude and bare,

As with joy they hailed its light, Leading onward, beaming bright;
There to bend the knee before Him whom heaven and earth adore;
So may we with holy joy, Pure and free from sin's alloy,

So, most gracious Lord, may we Evermore be led to Thee.
So may we with willing feet Ever seek Thy mercy seat.
All our costliest treasures bring, Christ, to Thee, our heav'nly King.

48

Angels from the Realms of Glory

James Montgomery, 1816

Henry Smart, 1867

Moderato

1. An-gels, from the realms of glo-ry, Wing your flight o'er all the earth,
2. Shep-herds in the field a-bid-ing, Watch-ing o'er your flocks by night,
3. Sag-es, leave your con-tem-pla-tions, Bright-er vi-sions beam a-far;

Ye, who sang cre-a-tion's sto-ry, Now pro-claim Mes-si-ah's birth.
God with man is now re-sid-ing, Yon-der shines the in-fant Light.
Seek the great De-sire of na-tions Ye have seen his na-tal star.

Come and wor-ship! Come and wor-ship! Wor-ship Christ the new-born King!

Masters in This Hall

William Morris, ca 1860

Carol from Chartres [WE]

Allegro moderato

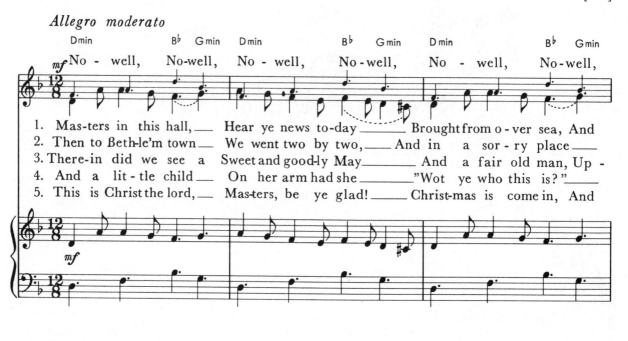

No - well, No-well, No - well, No-well, No - well, No-well,

1. Mas-ters in this hall,___ Hear ye news to-day___ Brought from o - ver sea, And
2. Then to Beth-le'm town___ We went two by two,___ And in a sor - ry place___
3. There-in did we see a Sweet and good-ly May___ And a fair old man, Up-
4. And a lit - tle child___ On her arm had she___ "Wot ye who this is?"___
5. This is Christ the lord,___ Mas-ters, be ye glad!___ Christ-mas is come in, And

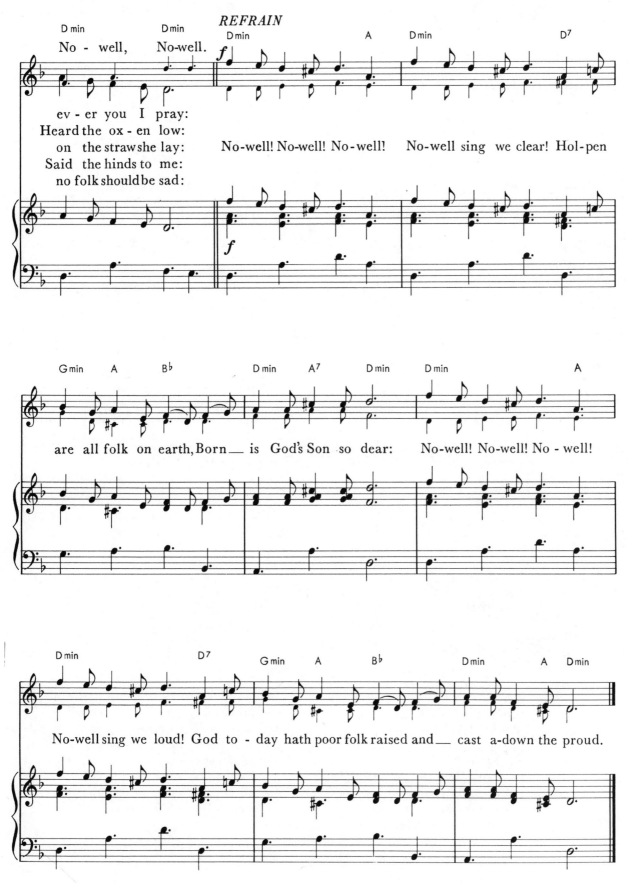

I Saw Three Ships

Traditional English

Traditional English
Arrangement: John Stainer

Allegretto moderato

1. I saw three ships come sail - ing in,
2. And what was in those ships all three?
3. Our Sav - ior Christ and His la - dy.
4. Pray, whith - er sailed those ships all three?

On

Christ - mas Day, on Christ - mas Day;

I saw three ships come
And what was in those
Our Sav - ior Christ and
Pray, whith - er sailed those

sail - ing in,
ships all three?
His la - dy,
ships all three?

On Christ - mas Day in the morn - ing.

5. O, they sailed in to Bethlehem, On Christmas Day, on Christmas Day,
O, they sailed in to Bethlehem, On Christmas Day in the morning.

6. And all the bells on earth shall ring, On
Christmas Day, on Christmas Day,
And all the bells on earth shall ring, On
Christmas Day in the morning.

7. And all the angels in Heav'n shall sing,
On Christmas Day, on Christmas Day,
And all the angels in Heav'n shall sing,
On Christmas Day in the morning.

8. And all the souls on earth shall sing, On
Christmas Day, on Christmas Day,
And all the souls on earth shall sing, On
Christmas Day in the morning.

9. Then let us all rejoice amain! On Christmas Day, on Christmas Day,
Then let us all rejoice amain! On Christmas Day in the morning.

DECK THE HALL
WITH BOUGHS OF HOLLY

Traditional Welsh

Old Welsh Carol

Allegro

1. Deck the hall with boughs of hol - ly,
2. See the blaz - ing Yule be - fore us,
3. Fast a - way the old year pass - es,

Fa la la la la, la la la la,

'Tis the sea - son to be jol - ly,
Strike the harp and join the cho - rus,
Hail the new, ye lads and lass - es,

Fa la la la la, la la la la.

Don we now our gay ap - par - rel,
Fol - low me in mer - ry meas - ure,
Sing we joy - ous all to - geth - er,

Fa__ la la__ la la la la,

Troll the an - cient Yule - tide car - ol,
While I tell of Yule - tide treas - ure,
Heed - less of the wind and weath - er,

Fa la la la la la la la la.

53

THE SNOW LAY ON THE GROUND

Traditional English, ca 1860

Traditional Irish - English Carol [WE]

Andante con moto

1. The snow lay on the ground, The star shone bright,___ When
2. 'Twas Ma - ry, Vir - gin pure, Of ho - ly Anne,___ That
3. Saint Jo - seph, too, was by To tend the Child; ___ To

Christ our Lord was born On Christ - mas night.___ Ve -
brought in - to this world On the God made Man.___ She
guard Him and pro - tect His Moth - er mild;___ The

ni - te a - do - re - mus Do - mi - num;___ Ve -
laid Him in a stall At Beth - le - hem,___ The
an - gels hov - ered round, And sang this song:___ Ve -

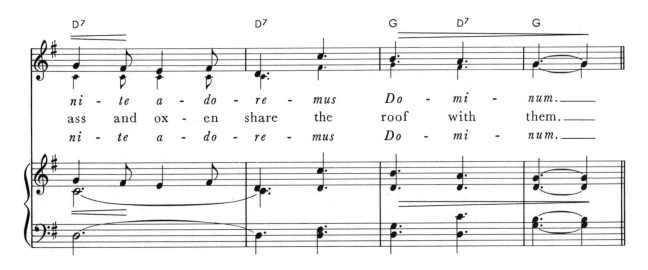

ni - te a - do - re - mus Do - mi - num._____
ass and ox - en share the roof with them._____
ni - te a - do - re - mus Do - mi - num._____

REFRAIN

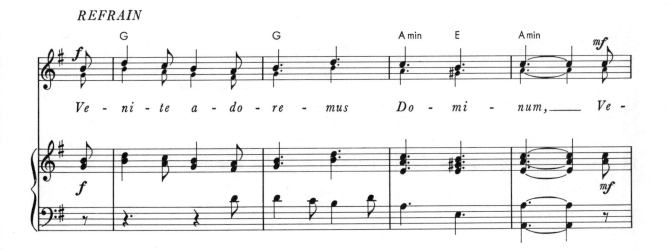

Ve - ni - te a - do - re - mus Do - mi - num,_____ Ve -

ni - te a - do - re - mus Do - mi - num._____

Baloo, Lammy

Traditional Scottish   17th Century Scottish   [WE]

1. This day to you is born a Child, Of Mary meek, the Virgin mild; That blessed Bairn so loving and kind, Shall now re-

2. And now shall Mary's little Boy, For-ev-er be our Hope and Joy; E-ter-nal be His reign on earth, Re-joice, then all

3. Sleep gent-ly, King Jesus, and know no fear, Thy sub-jects a-dor-ing, watch o-ver Thee here, God's an-gels and shep-herds, and kine in their stall, And wise men and

56

joice——— both heart —— and—— mind;
peo - ple, for this—— ho-ly birth; } Ba - loo,—— Lam - my.
Vir - gin, Thy guar - dians—— all;

I HEARD THE BELLS ON CHRISTMAS DAY

Henry W. Longfellow, 1863   J. Baptiste Calkin, 1872

1. I heard the bells on Christ-mas day Their
2. I thought how, as the day had come, The
3. And in de-spair I bow'd my head: "There
4. Then pealed the bells more loud and deep: "God

old fa-mil-iar car-ols play, And wild and sweet the
bel-fries of all Christ-en-dom Had roll'd a-long th'un
is no peace on earth," I said, "For hate is strong and
is not dead, nor doth He sleep; The wrong shall fail, the

words re-peat Of peace on earth, good will to men.
bro-ken song Of peace on earth, good will to men.
mocks the song Of peace on earth, good will to men."
right pre-vail, With peace on earth, good will to men."

ALL MY HEART THIS NIGHT REJOICES*

Paulus Gerhardt, 1656
Translation: Catherine Winkworth

Horatio Parker, 1894 [WE]

Allegretto

1. All my heart this night re-joi-ces, As I hear, far and near,
Sweet-est an-gel voi-ces; "Christ is born," their choirs are sing-ing,
Till the air, Ev-'ry-where, Now with joy is ring-ing.

2. Hark! a voice from yon-der man-ger, Soft and sweet, doth en-treat,
"Flee from woe and dan-ger. Breth-ren, come; from all that grieves you,
You are freed, All you need I will sure-ly give you."

3. Come, then, let us has-ten yon-der; Here let all, great and small,
Kneel in awe and won-der. Love Him who with love is yearn-ing,
Hail the star That from far Bright with hope is burn-ing!

*The German text for this carol may be found on page **320**.

AWAY IN A MANGER

Anonymous

J.R. Murray, 1877 [WE]

1. A - way in a man - ger, no crib for a bed, The lit - tle Lord Je - sus laid down His sweet head. The stars in the sky——— looked down where He lay, The lit - tle Lord Je sus, a - sleep on the hay.
2. The cat - tle are low - ing, the Ba - by a - wakes, But lit - tle Lord Je - sus, no cry - ing He makes. I love Thee, Lord Je - sus, look down from the sky, And stay by my cra - dle till morn - ing is nigh.
3. Be near me, Lord Je - sus, I ask Thee to stay Close by me for - ev - er, and love me, I pray. Bless all the dear chil - dren in Thy ten - der care, And fit us for Heav - en to live with Thee there.

There's a Song in the Air

Josiah G. Holland, 1879

Karl P. Harrington, 1905

Allegretto moderato

1. There's a song in the air! There's a star in the sky! There's a moth-er's deep prayer And a ba-by's low cry! And the star rains its fire while the beau-ti-ful sing, For the man-ger of Beth-le-hem cra-dles a King!

2. There's a tu-mult of joy O'er the won-der-ful birth, For the Vir-gin's sweet boy Is the Lord of the earth. Ay! the star rains its fire while the beau-ti-ful sing, For the man-ger of Beth-le-hem cra-dles a King!

3. In the light of that star Lie the a-ges im-pearled, And that song from a-far Has swept o-ver the world. Ev-'ry hearth is a-flame, and the beau-ti-ful sing, In the homes of the na-tions that Je-sus is King!

4. We re-joice in the light, And we ech-o the song That comes down thro' the night From the heav-en-ly throng. Ay! we shout to the love-ly e-van-gel they bring, And we greet in His cra-dle our Sav-ior and King!

It Came upon the Midnight Clear

Edmund H. Sears, 1846 alt.

Richard S. Willis, 1850

Andante

1. It came up-on the mid-night clear, That glo-rious song of old, From
2. Still through the clo-ven skies they come, With peace-ful wings un-furl'd, And
3. O ye, be-neath life's crush-ing load, Whose forms are bend-ing low, Who
4. For lo! the days are has-t'ning on, By proph-ets seen of old, When

an-gels bend-ing near the earth, To touch their harps of gold, "Peace
still their heav'n-ly mu-sic floats O'er all the wear-y world: A-
toil a-long the climb-ing way With pain-ful steps and slow: Look
with the ev-er cir-cling years, Shall come the time fore-told, When

on the earth, good will to men From heav'n's all gra-cious King." The
bove its sad and low-ly plains They bend on hov-'ring wing. And
now, for glad and gold-en hours Come swift-ly on the wing; Oh
peace shall o-ver all the earth Its an-cient splen-dors fling, And

world in sol-emn still-ness lay, To hear the an-gels sing.
ev-er o'er its Ba-bel sounds The bless-ed an-gels sing.
rest be-side the wear-y road And hear the an-gels sing.
the whole world send back the song Which now the an-gels sing.

62

O LITTLE TOWN OF BETHLEHEM

Phillips Brooks, 1868-1893

Lewis H. Redner, 1868-1908 [WE]

1. O lit - tle town of Beth - le - hem, How still we see thee lie! A-
2. For Christ is born of Ma - ry, And gath-ered all a - bove, While
3. How si - lent - ly, how si - lent - ly The won-drous gift is given! So
4. O ho - ly Child of Beth - le - hem! De - scend to us, we pray; Cast

bove thy deep and dream-less sleep The si - lent stars go by; Yet
mor-tals sleep, the an - gels keep Their watch of won-d'ring love. O
God im-parts to hu - man hearts The bless-ings of His heaven. No
out our sin and en - ter in, Be born in us to - day. We

in thy dark streets shin - eth The ev - er - last - ing Light; The
morn - ing stars to - geth - er Pro - claim the ho - ly birth, And
ear may hear His com - ing, But in this world of sin, Where
hear the Christ-mas an - gels The great glad tid - ings tell; O

hopes and fears of all the years Are met in thee to - night.
prais - es sing to God the King, And peace to men on earth!
meek souls will re - ceive Him still, The dear Christ en - ters in.
come to us, a - bide with us, Our Lord Im - man - u - el!

Everywhere, Everywhere, Christmas Tonight

Phillips Brooks, 1835–1893

Lewis H. Redner, 1831–1908 [WE]

Moderato

1. Christ-mas in lands of the fir tree and pine, Christ-mas in lands of the palm tree and vine, Christ-mas where snow peaks stand

2. Christ-mas where chil-dren are hope-ful and gay, Christ-mas where old men are pa-tient and gray, Christ-mas where peace like a

sol - emn and white Christ - mas where corn - fields lie sun - ny and
dove in its flight Broods o'er brave men in the thick of the

bright. Ev - 'ry - where, ev - 'ry - where, Christ - mas to - night.
fight. Ev - 'ry - where, ev - 'ry - where, Christ - mas to - night.

We Three Kings of Orient Are

John H. Hopkins, 1857

John H. Hopkins, 1857

REFRAIN

O— star of won-der, star of night, Star with roy-al beau-ty bright,

West-ward lead-ing still pro-ceed-ing, Guide us to Thy per-fect light.

Gather around the Christmas Tree

John H. Hopkins

John H. Hopkins, 1820–1891 [WE]

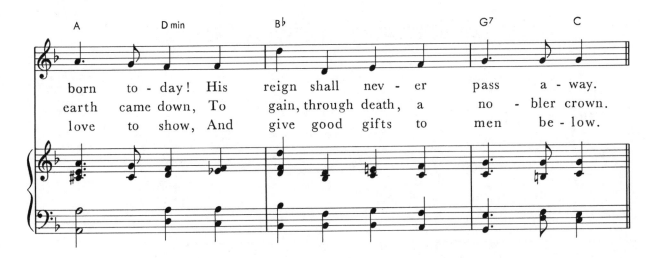

born to-day! His reign shall nev-er pass a-way.
earth came down, To gain, through death, a no-bler crown.
love to show, And give good gifts to men be-low.

REFRAIN

Ho - san - na, Ho - san - na, Ho - san - na, in the high-est!

JINGLE BELLS

James Pierpont

James Pierpont [WE]

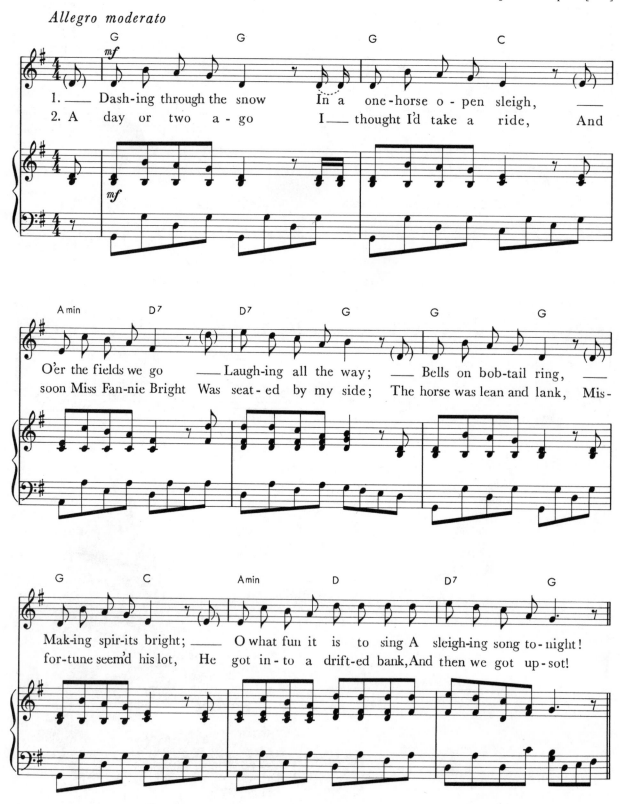

1. ___ Dash-ing through the snow In a one-horse o-pen sleigh, ___
2. A day or two a-go I ___ thought I'd take a ride, And

O'er the fields we go ___ Laugh-ing all the way; ___ Bells on bob-tail ring, ___
soon Miss Fan-nie Bright Was seat-ed by my side; The horse was lean and lank, Mis-

Mak-ing spir-its bright; ___ O what fun it is to sing A sleigh-ing song to-night!
for-tune seem'd his lot, He got in-to a drift-ed bank, And then we got up-sot!

REFRAIN

Up on the Housetop

B.R. Hanby

B.R. Hanby [WE]

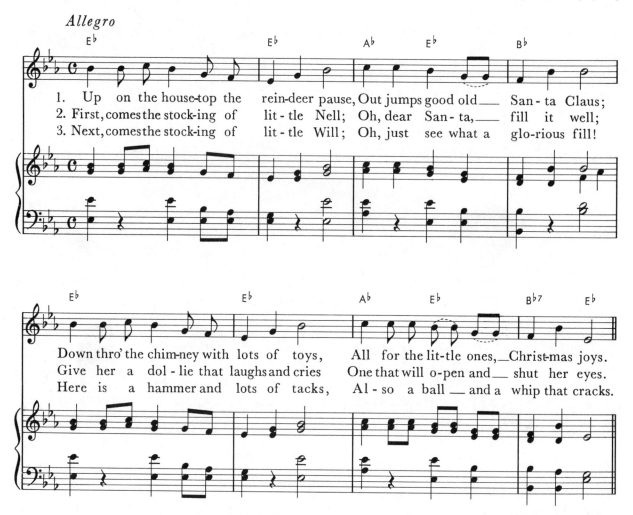

Allegro

1. Up on the house-top the rein-deer pause, Out jumps good old__ San-ta Claus;
2. First, comes the stock-ing of lit-tle Nell; Oh, dear San-ta,__ fill it well;
3. Next, comes the stock-ing of lit-tle Will; Oh, just see what a glo-rious fill!

Down thro' the chim-ney with lots of toys, All for the lit-tle ones,__ Christ-mas joys.
Give her a dol-lie that laughs and cries One that will o-pen and__ shut her eyes.
Here is a hammer and lots of tacks, Al-so a ball__ and a whip that cracks.

REFRAIN

Ho, ho, ho! who wouldn't go! Ho, ho, ho! who wouldn't go! ——

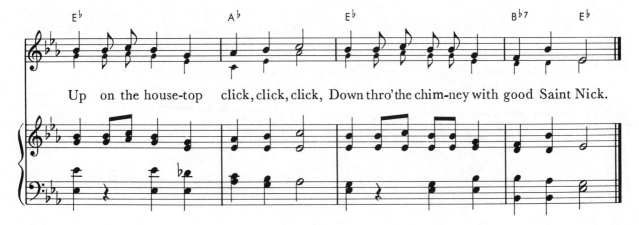

Up on the house-top click, click, click, Down thro'the chim-ney with good Saint Nick.

73

JOLLY OLD SAINT NICHOLAS

Traditional United States

Traditional United States [WE]

Allegretto con moto

1. Jol - ly old Saint Nich - o - las, Lean your ear this way!
2. When the clock is strik - ing twelve, When I'm fast a - sleep,
3. John - ny wants a pair of skates; Su - sy wants a sled;

Don't you tell a sin - gle soul What I'm going to say;
Down the chim - ney broad and black, With your pack you'll creep;
Nel - lie wants a pic - ture book Yel - low, blue, and red;

Christ-mas Eve is com - ing soon; Now, my dear old man,
All the stock-ings you will find Hang -ing in a row;
Now I think I'll leave to you What to give the rest;

Whis - per what you'll bring to me, Tell me, if you can.
Mine will be the short-est one, You'll be sure to know.
Choose for me, dear San - ta Claus, You will know the best.

75

The Winter Moon Shone Cold and Clear

Original words in Huron Indian
by Father Jean de Brebeuf, 1593–1649
English paraphrase [GKE]

Andante

Es - ten - ni - a - lon de tso - nu - e Ie - sus a - ha -
The win - ter moon shone cold and clear When Je - sus Christ was

ton - ni - a, On na - u - a - te - ua 'd'o - ki n'on -
born ———, Then Git - chi Man - i - tou sent sing - ing

an - das - kua - en - tak; En - on - chi - en skua -
an - gels from His throne; Their shin - ing robes be -

tri - ho - tat h'o - nu - an - di - lon - ra - cha - tha——:
dimmed each star, **And** marv - 'ling hun - ters heard the choir——:

REFRAIN

"Ie - sus a - ha - ton - ni - a, a - ha - ton - ni -
"Now—— is Sal - va - tion come, Je—— sus is

a; Ie - sus a - ha - ton - ni - a."
born; Je - sus Christ the Lord is born."

BEHOLD THAT STAR

Thomas W. Talley

Thomas W. Talley [WE]

Be - hold that star!___ Be - hold___ that star up yon - der,

Be - hold that star!___ It is the star of Beth - le - hem.___

VERSE

Cmin   B♭7   E♭

It is the star of Beth-le-hem.

1. There was no room found in the inn _____ For
2. The wise men trav - elled from the East _____ To
3. A song broke forth up - on the night _____ From

Cmin   B♭7   E♭

It is the star of Beth-le-hem.

Him who was born free from sin. _____ Oh,
wor-ship Him, the Prince of Peace. _____ Oh,
an-gel hosts all robed in white. _____ Oh,

D.C.

D.C.

79

Rise Up, Shepherd, and Follow*

Traditional Spiritual

Traditional Spiritual [WE]

1. There's a star in the East on — Christ-mas Morn,
2. If you take good — heed to the an-gel's word,

Rise up, shep-herd, and fol-low

It will
You'll for-

lead to the place where the Sav-ior's born; —
get your — flock, you'll for-get your herd; —

Rise up, shep-herd, and fol-low. —

REFRAIN

Leave your ewes and leave your lambs, Rise up, shep-herd, and fol-low, —

* Words to verses may be sung by a soloist, with all voices singing
"Rise up, shepherd, and follow" as a response.

Children, Go Where I Send Thee

Traditional Spiritual

Traditional United States [WE]

4. Four for the four that stood at the door.
5. Five for the gospel preachers.
6. Six for the six that never got fixed.
7. Sev'n for the sev'n that never went to Heav'n.
8. Eight for the eight that stood at the gate.
9. Nine for the nine that dressed so fine.
10. Ten for the Ten Commandments.

* Sing these two measures two times for verse 2, three times for verse 3, etc.
Verses accumulate in reverse order.

MARY HAD A BABY

Traditional Spiritual

Traditional Spiritual [WE]

Go Tell It on the Mountain

Traditional Spiritual

Traditional Spiritual [WE]

Allegretto moderato

REFRAIN

Go tell it on the moun-tain, ev-'ry-where; —

Go tell it on the moun-tain, O-ver the hills and ev-'ry-where; —

Go tell it on the moun-tain, Christ is born. *Fine*

Go tell it on the moun-tain, That Je-sus Christ is born. *Fine*

VERSE

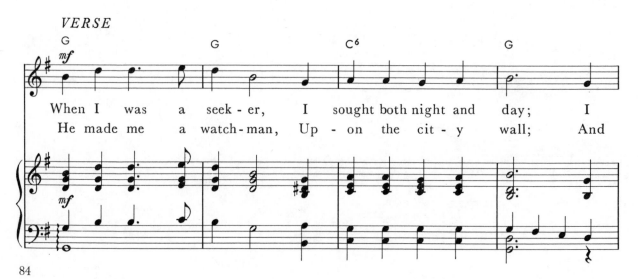

When I was a seek-er, I sought both night and day; I

He made me a watch-man, Up-on the cit-y wall; And

84

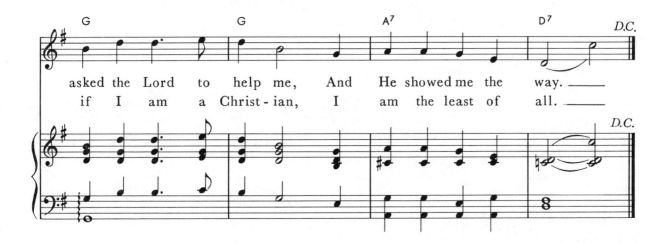

asked the Lord to help me, And He showed me the way. _____
if I am a Christ - ian, I am the least of all. _____

O PO' LITTLE JESUS

Traditional Spiritual

Traditional Spiritual [WE]

By permission of copyright owners, Lawson-Gould Music Pub., Inc.

Hush, My Babe, Lie Still and Slumber

Isaac Watts, 1674–1748

Kentucky Carol [WE]

Larghetto

1. Hush, my babe, lie still and slum - ber,
2. How much bet - ter art thou at - tend - ed
3. Soft and eas - y is thy cra - dle,

Ho - ly an - gels guard thy bed, Heav'n - ly bless - ings
Than the Son of God could be When from Heav - en
Coarse and hard the Sav - ior lay, When His birth - place

with - out num - ber gent - ly steal - ing on thy head.
He de - scend - ed, And be - came a Child like thee.
was a sta - ble, And His soft - est bed was hay.

BRIGHTEST AND BEST

(Star of the East)

Reginald Heber (alt)

United States Folk Hymn [WE]

Andante

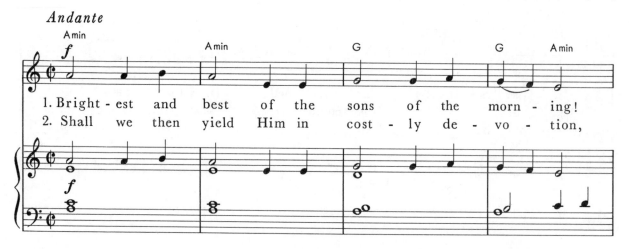

1. Bright-est and best of the sons of the morn - ing!
2. Shall we then yield Him in cost - ly de - vo - tion,

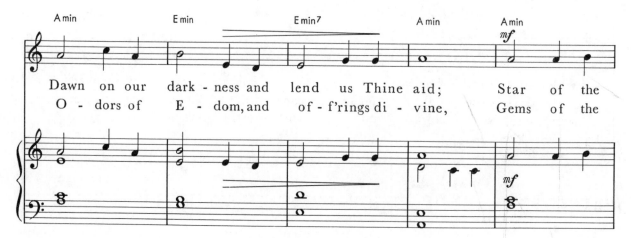

Dawn on our dark-ness and lend us Thine aid;   Star of the
O - dors of E - dom, and of - f'rings di - vine,   Gems of the

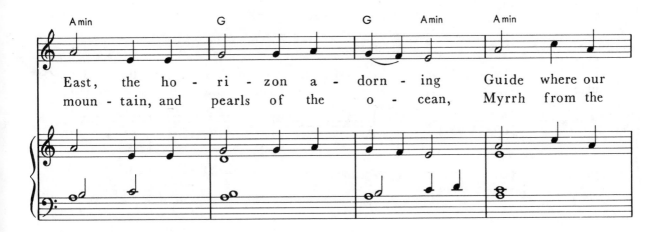

East, the ho - ri - zon a - dorn - ing Guide where our
moun - tain, and pearls of the o - cean, Myrrh from the

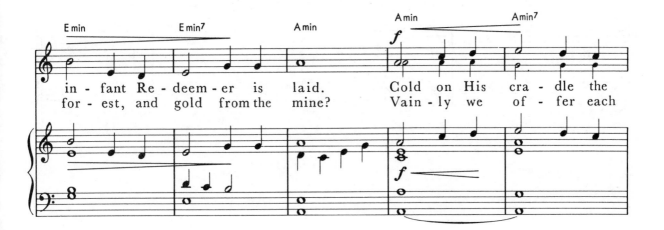

in - fant Re - deem - er is laid. Cold on His cra - dle the
for - est, and gold from the mine? Vain - ly we of - fer each

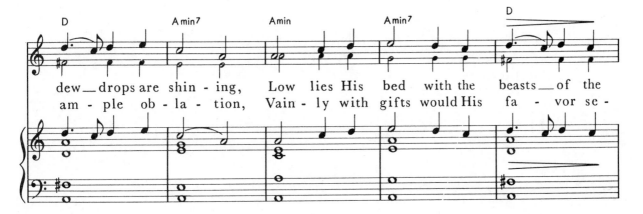

dew __ drops are shin - ing, Low lies His bed with the beasts __ of the
am - ple ob - la - tion, Vain - ly with gifts would His fa - vor se -

stall;   An - gels a - dore Him in slum - ber re - clin - ing,
cure;   Rich - er by far is the heart's ad - o - ra - tion,

Mak - er and Mon - arch and Sav - ior of all.
Dear - er to God are the prayers of the poor.

FRENCH CAROLS

CÉLÉBRONS LA NAISSANCE
WE SING IN CELEBRATION

Traditional French [GKE]

15th Century French [WE]

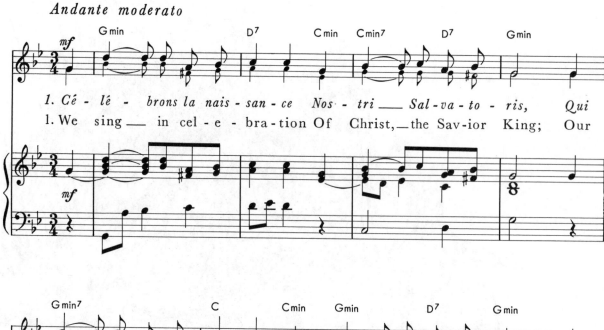

Andante moderato

1. Cé - lé - brons la nais - san - ce Nos - tri __ Sal - va - to - ris, Qui
1. We sing __ in cel - e - bra - tion Of Christ, __ the Sav - ior King; Our

fait __ la com - plai - san - ce De - i __ su - i Pa - tris, Cet
Hope __ and Ju - bi - la - tion, Whom God __ to earth doth bring; This

en - fant tout ai - ma - ble, In noc - te me - di - â. Est
Babe, __ so sweet and gen - tle, That came __ to earth this night, Is

92

né ___ dans une é - ta - ble De cas - ta Ma - ri - a.
born ___ with-in a sta - ble To Ma - ry, Vir-gin mild.

2. *Cette heureuse nouvelle*
   Olim pastoribus
   Par un ange fidèle
   Fuit nuntiatus,
   Leur disant laissez paître
   In agro viridi
   Venez voir votre maître
   Filium que Dei.

3. *A cette voix céleste,*
   Omnes hi Pastores,
   D'un air doux et modeste
   Et multum gaudentes,
   Incontinent marchèrent
   Relicto pecore.
   Tous ensemble arriverent
   In Bethlehem Judae.

4. *Mille esprits angéliques,*
   Sancti pastoribus,
   Chantent dans leur musique,
   Puer vobis natus,
   Au Dieu par qui nous sommes,
   Gloria in excelsis,
   Et la paix soit aux hommes
   Bonae voluntatis.

2. The shepherds on the hillside
   Were watching o'er their sheep,
   When there appeared an angel
   From out the darkness deep,
   Announcing that the Baby,
   Who in the manger lay,
   Was God, the Heav'nly Father,
   Who came to earth today.

3. To hear the heav'nly tidings,
   The shepherds all rejoiced;
   And, filled with awe and wonder,
   Their great thanksgiving voiced.
   Together they came running,
   Unheeding of their flocks,
   To see the holy Infant
   That Mary holds and rocks.

4. The angels from the Highest
   Burst forth in sweetest song;
   And soon the shepherds joined them
   With voices clear and strong:
   "To God, our Heav'nly Father,
   All praise and glory be;
   On earth His peace bestowing,
   Good will, eternally."

Il Est Né, le Divin Enfant
HE IS BORN, THE HOLY CHILD

Traditional 19th Century French [GKE]

18th Century French Carol [WE]

Allegretto
REFRAIN

1. Il est né, le di-vin En-fant, Jou-ez haut-
1. He is born, the ___ ho-ly Child, Play the ___

bois, ré-son-nez mu-set-tes! Il est né, le di-
o-boe and bag-pipes mer-ri-ly! He is born, the ___

vin En-fant, Chan-tons tous son a-vè-ne-ment!
ho-ly Child, Sing we all of the Sav-ior mild.

Fine

2. *Ah! qu'il est beau, qu'il est charmant,*
   Ah! que ses grâces sont parfaites!
   Ah! qu'il est beau, qu'il est charmant,
   Qu'il est doux, ce divin Enfant!
       Refrain

2. O how lovely, O how pure,
   Is this perfect Child of Heaven;
   O how lovely, O how pure,
   Gracious gift of God to man!
       Refrain

3. *Ô Jesus, Ô Roi tout puissant,*
   Si petit Enfant que vous êtes,
   Ô Jesus, Ô Roi tout puissant,
   Regnez sur nous entièrement.
       Refrain

3. Jesus, Lord of all the world,
   Coming as a Child among us,
   Jesus, Lord of all the world,
   Grant to us Thy heav'nly peace.
       Refrain

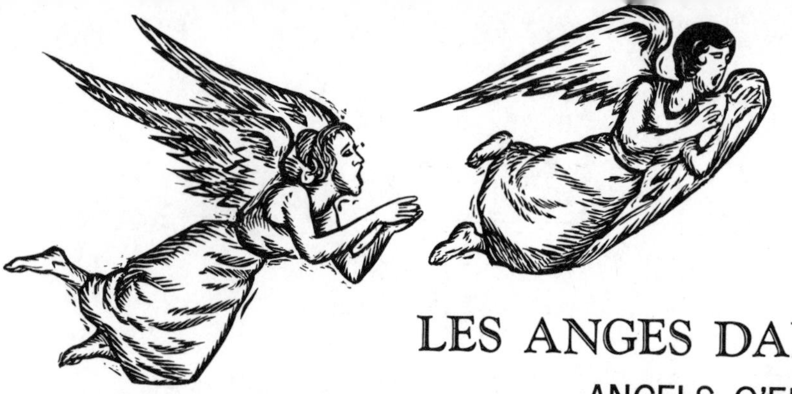

LES ANGES DANS NOS CAMPAGNES

ANGELS O'ER THE FIELDS WERE SINGING

Traditional French [GKE]

19th Century French Carol [WE]

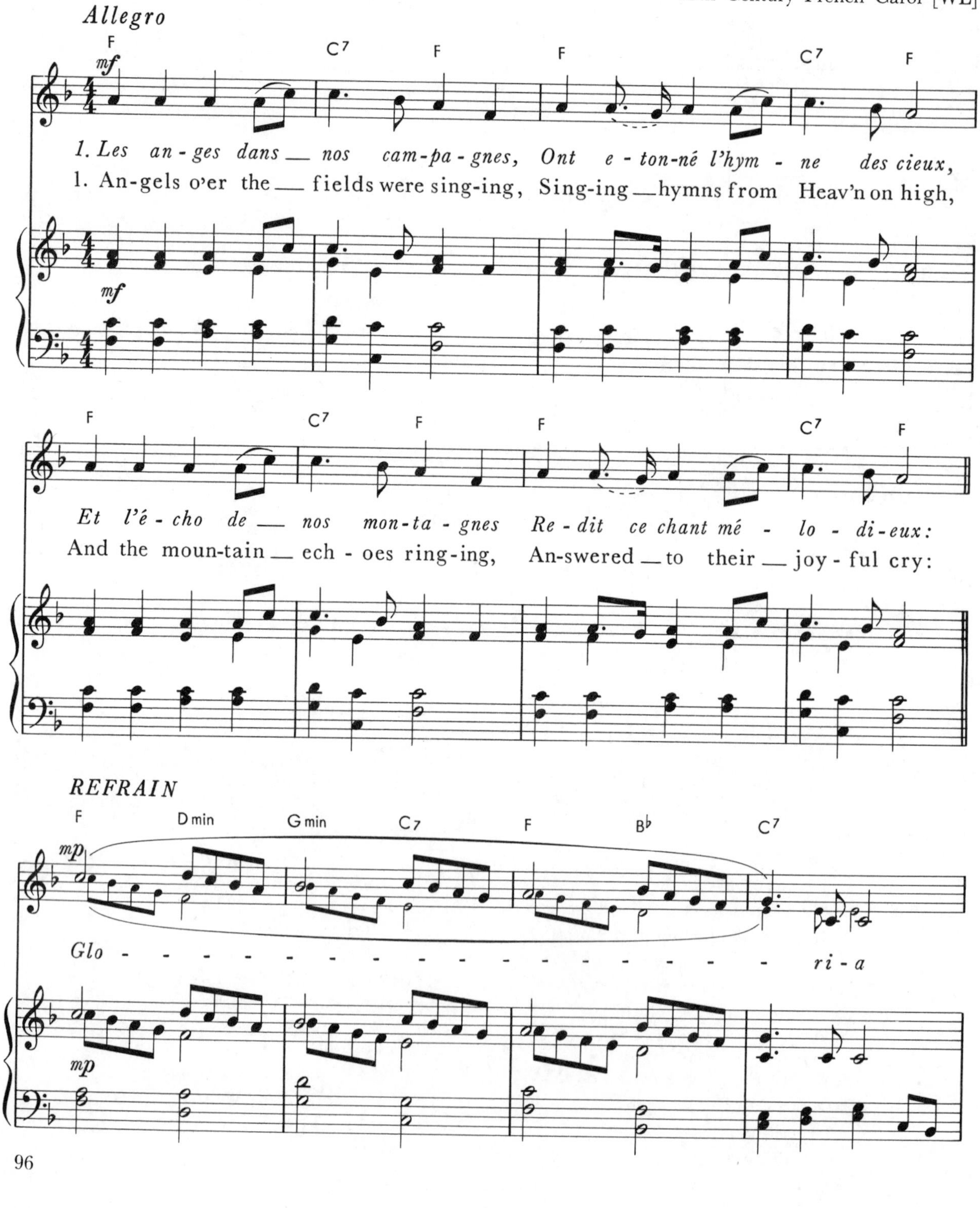
Allegro
F C7 F F C7 F
mf
1. Les an-ges dans nos cam-pa-gnes, Ont e-ton-né l'hym-ne des cieux,
1. An-gels o'er the fields were sing-ing, Sing-ing hymns from Heav'n on high,
mf
F C7 F F C7 F
Et l'é-cho de nos mon-ta-gnes Re-dit ce chant mé-lo-di-eux:
And the moun-tain ech-oes ring-ing, An-swered to their joy-ful cry:
REFRAIN
F Dmin Gmin C7 F B♭ C7
mp
Glo - - - - - - - - - - - - - - - - - - - ri-a
mp

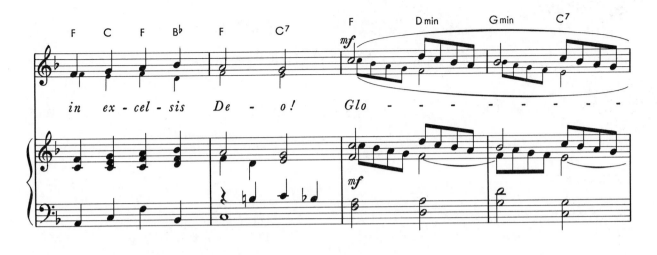

in ex - cel - sis De - o! Glo - - - - - - - -

- - - - - ri - a in ex - cel - sis De - - o!

2. *Bergers, pour qui cette fête!*
   Quel est l'objet de tous ces chants?
   Quel vainqueur, quelle conquête
   Mérite ces cris triomphants?
     Refrain

3. *Ils annoncent la naissance*
   Du libérateur d'Israël,
   Et, pleins de reconnaissance,
   Chantent en ce jour solennel:
     Refrain

4. *Cherchons tous l'heureux village*
   Qui l'a vu naître sous ses toits;
   Offrons-lui le tendre hommage
   Et de nos coeurs et de nos voix!
     Refrain

2. Shepherds, why this celebration?
   Why this burst of heav'nly song?
   What could cause such jubilation?
   What inspired the heav'nly throng?
     Refrain

3. They are bringing wond'rous tidings,
   Tidings of an infant King
   Who will bring us peace abiding,
   'Tis of Jesus Christ they sing.
     Refrain

4. We will seek the happy village
   Of His birth this holy day,
   We will offer deepest homage
   As our hearts and voices say:
     Refrain

QUITTEZ, PASTEURS
O COME AWAY, YE SHEPHERDS

18th Century French [GKE]　　　　　　　　　From air, "Nanon Dormait," 1875 [WE]

Allegretto con moto

1. Quit - tez, pas - teurs, vos bre - bis, vos hou -
1. O come a - way, ye shep herds, leave your

let - tes, Vo - tre ha - meau Et le soin du trou -
sheep!___ A King has come to ease our woe so

peau;___ Chan - gez vos pleurs en u - ne joie par -
deep!___ O change your tears To praise and ju - bi -

THE CATHOLICS
OF
HARVARD SQUARE

edited by
JEFFREY WILLS

SAINT BEDE'S PUBLICATIONS

282.7444 C2869h 1993

The Catholics of Harvard
  Square   FEB 0 1 '10

282.744
W 741

Saint Bede's Publications
P.O. Box 545, Petersham, MA 01366

© 1993 by Jeffrey Wills. All rights reserved.
Printed in the United States of America

97 96 95 94 93   5 4 3 2 1

Paper ISBN: 1-879007-00-2
Cloth ISBN: 1-879007-01-0

PHOTO CREDITS

Most of the illustrations in this volume come from the files of St.
Paul's Parish and the Harvard-Radcliffe Catholic Student Center,
or were photographed by the editor. Unfortunately, in most
cases the name of the original photographer or artist is now
unknown and cannot be properly credited. The publishers are
particularly grateful to the following individuals and institutions
for permission to reproduce photographic material on the following pages:

Abbey of Gethsemani, Kentucky: 93
Archives of the Archdiocese of Boston: 36-37, 39-40, 55, 56, 59, 63,
100 (Sr. Rita Murray)
Cambridge Historical Society: 8, 20-21, 71, 104, 140
Georgetown University Special Collections: 66, 83
Harvard University Archives: 57, 61, 62 (both), 69, 70, 72, 74, 77,
78, 79, 88, 89, 120, 136
Harvard University News Office: 101 (Jane Reed), 191
Maryknoll: 42
Radcliffe College Archives: 107 (both), 109, 112, 114, 115, 141
Sisters of St. Joseph, Brighton: 32
University of Notre Dame Archives: 68, 81, 84, 93
University of Wisconsin Archives: 110, 111
Harry Brett (Image Photos): 96, 124, 153, 190
William Mercer: 18, 50, 123, 164, 173, 189
Francis Bane: 151, 157
Marie Costello: 134
Elizabeth Linehan: 34
Genevieve Mathison: 129, 131

8785

PREFACE

Two apostles diverse in background but single in purpose face each other across the nave of Harvard Square's Catholic Church—St. Peter and St. Paul. Donated respectively by the Knights of Columbus and the Harvard Catholic Club, this pair of statues embodies a unity of town and gown in worship, if nothing else. When the first wooden Church of St. Paul was dedicated in 1875, the mainly Irish parish of immigrants had little religious interaction with the Protestant college. But when its mighty Romanesque successor was completed fifty years later, the now prospering community felt confident enough to preach an educational sermon to its famous neighbor. Throughout the church's windows, murals and brickwork is proclaimed the message that here the pursuits of faith and truth are inseparable. That conviction has since been confirmed, as Catholics have entered the university in great numbers while Harvard has intermingled with the neighborhood.

At one time the effort of the Catholic Church in this place was to establish a family parish for a large needy population of immigrants, while leaving the university uncultivated. Gradually, as the university grew and changed complexion, the Catholics at Harvard proved themselves to be not only faithful to the Church, but inspirational to non-Catholics. In this evangelization the local Catholic citizenry, both at work and at prayer, were allies. As long as Harvard Square remains a sophisticated center of learning, St. Paul's mission is to be the presence of the Catholic Church in that educated community.

Unlike many urban parishes, changes for St. Paul's did not mean decline. First, the community which built the church also built a rich liturgical tradition which more than ever attracts worshipers from the entire Boston area. Secondly, as the immigrant community receded, the parish adapted itself to the growing number of Catholic students and staff at Harvard and Radcliffe. The continuing commitment to integrated Christian service, education and the arts was especially witnessed and renewed in the combination of parish halls, student chaplaincy and choir school in the St. Paul Center of 1991—collaborative components of a single community seeking faith and learning. This book traces the interlocking history of those components.

This publication is partly a history, partly a collection of sources—a primary record of the various Catholic experiences of a particular place, intended to have an immediacy that will intrigue the present generation to discover its roots. We have taken the time of the Second Vatican Council as our climax, with only brief remarks about the subsequent generation. It is that present generation, however, which has been the sturdy "pillar and ground" of this endeavor. That support was made incarnate on endless occasions by Rev. John Boles and the staffs of St. Paul's Parish, the Harvard-

Radcliffe Catholic Student Center and the Boston Archdiocesan Choir School, who dug through drawers and closets for photographs, read various versions of the manuscript, and always allowed us a free hand.

Of the many others to be thanked for the final result, only a few can be named here. First, the collaborating authors donated their patience as well as their words, particularly Marie Daly who made numerous trips to record interviews. In addition to those conversations printed here, interviews were kindly granted by Walter Sullivan, Edward Sullivan, Agnes Mongan, and Christopher Huntington. This book could not have been assembled without the assistance of many archivists: Ron Patkus and Phyllis Danehy at the Archdiocese of Boston, Robin McElheny and the staff at Harvard, Jane Knowles at Radcliffe, Jon Reynolds and Nicholas Sheets at Georgetown, Peter Lysy and Charles Lamb at Notre Dame, Kelly Fitzpatrick at Mt. St. Mary's, Sr. Blaithin Sullivan at the Boston Sisters of St. Joseph, and Charles Sullivan at the Cambridge Historical Commission. Also helpful were correspondence and conversations with Leo Abbot, Frank Bannon, Dennis Crowley, Rev. Emmet Curran, S.J., Marian Desrosiers, Rev. John Whitney Evans, and Joan Keenan.

In early stages of processing the text and photos, Anh Nguyen, Tom Winslow, and Michael Skinner donated their time; in the later stages, Susan Ryan provided a trained writer's eyes and encouraged substantial revisions. Coping with an absent editor, Mary MacMillen and Michael Michaud were undaunted allies to the end; they alone know what thanks they are owed for a series of minor miracles.

faite; Al - lez tous a - do - rer / la - tion! We jour-ney to a - dore

Un Dieu, / A God,

Un Dieu, / A God,

Dieu, / God,

Un Dieu, Un Dieu qui vient vous con - so - ler. / A God, Who brings us con - so - la - tion.

2. *Vous le verrez*
   Couché dans une étable,
   Comme un enfant
   Nu, pauvre et languissant;
   Reconnaissez
   Son amour ineffable
   Pour nous venir chercher
   Il est, Il est,
   Il est le fidèle berger!

2. O see Him there,
   So naked, weak and helpless!
   A tiny babe
   Within a manger laid.
   From Heav'n above
   He comes to earth to save us
   As God's incarnate Word.
   He is, He is,
   Our Lord and faithful Shepherd.

Le Sommeil de l'Enfant Jésus
THE SLEEP OF THE INFANT JESUS

Traditional French [GKE]

Traditional French
Harmonized by François Gervaert, 1828–1908 [WE]

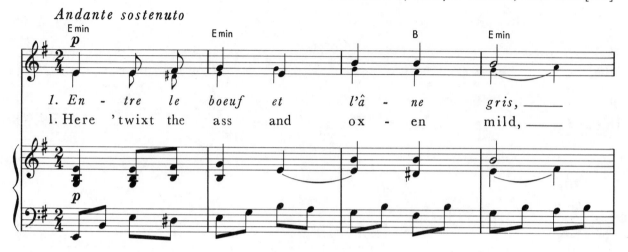

Andante sostenuto

1. En - tre le boeuf et l'â - ne gris, ____
1. Here 'twixt the ass and ox - en mild, ____

Dors, dors, dors le pe - tit fils:
Sleep, sleep, sleep, Thou lit - tle child:

Dors, ____ dors, ____ dors. ____
Sleep, ____ sleep, ____ sleep. ____

REFRAIN

Mille an - ges di - vins, *Mil - le se - ra - phins,*
An - gels pure and white, Guard Thee through the night,

Vo - lent à l'en - tour de ce grand Dieu d'a - mour.
Hov - 'ring o'er the cra - dle of the God of Light.

2. *Entre le roses et les lys,*
   Dors, dors, dors le petit fils:
   Refrain

2. Here, with the rose and lily bright,
   Sleep, sleep, sleep Thou little Child:
   Refrain

3. *Entre les pastoureaux jolis,*
   Dors, dors, dors le petit fils:
   Refrain

3. Here, 'mid the shepherds' great delight,
   Sleep, sleep, sleep Thou little Child:
   Refrain

Quelle Est Cette Odeur Agréable?
WHAT IS THIS PERFUME SO APPEALING?

Traditional French [GKE]   Traditional French [WE]

1. Quelle est cette o - deur a - gré - a - ble,
1. What is this per - fume so ap - peal - ing,

Ber - gers, qui ra - vit tous nos sens? S'ex - ha - le -
Shep - herds, that fills the win - ter air? Love - li - er

t - il rien de sem - bla - ble Au mi - lieu des fleurs
frag - rance ne'er came steal - ing From fields of spring - time

102

du prin - temps?____ Quelle est cette o - deur a - gré -
blos - soms fair!____ What is this per - fume so ap -

a - ble, Ber - gers, qui ra - vit tous nos sens?
peal - ing, Shep - herds, that fills the win - ter air?

2. *Mais quelle éclatante lumière*
Dans la nuit vient frapper nos yeux?
L'astre du jour dans sa carrière
Futil jamais si radieux!
Mais quelle éclatante lumière
Dans la nuit vient frapper nos yeux?

3. *A Bethléem dans une crèche*
Il vient de vous naître un Sauveur.
Allons que rien ne vous empêche
D'adorer votre Rédempteur.
A Bethléem dans une crèche
Il vient de vous naître un Sauveur.

2. What is this star so brightly shining
In the dark night, that blinds our sight?
Ne'er did the sun, at morning dawning,
Beam with more glorious, radiant light!
What is this star so brightly shining
In the dark night, that blinds our sight?

3. At Bethlehem, in lowly manger,
Is born to you an infant King;
Hasten to kneel beside your Savior,
Your praise and adoration bring.
At Bethlehem, in lowly manger,
Is born to you an infant King.

Quoi, Ma Voisine, Es-Tu Fâchée?

NEIGHBOR, WHAT HAS YOU SO EXCITED?

Traditional French [GKE]   Traditional French [WE]

1. Quoi, ma voi - sine, es - tu fâ - ché - e?
1. "Neigh - bor, what has you so ex - cit - ted?

Dis - moi pour - quoi, Veux - tu ve - nir voir
Do tell me, please." "Have -n't you heard? A

l'ac - cou - ché - e A - vec - que moi?
Boy is born that All want to see!

104

C'est u - ne da - me fort dis - crè - te,
Son of a pure and mod - est vir - gin,

Ce m'a-t-on dit, Qui nous a pro - duit
Ma - ry's her name, They say her Ba - by

le Pro - phè - te Sou - vent pré - dit.
is the Sav - ior Proph-ets pro - claim."

2. "Je le veux, allons, ma commère,
C'est mon désir,
Nous verrons l'enfant et la mère
Tout à loisir;
Aurons nous pas de la dragée
Et du gâteau?
La salle est-elle bien rangée?
Y fait-il beau?"

2. "It would be pleasant to go with you,
Likely I'll go.
But can't we take our time to see them?
Why hurry so?
Have you some cake to take the Infant?
Sugar-plums, too?
I'm sure that Mary's house is lovely,
Tidy and new."

3. *"Ah! ma bergère, tu te trompes*
Bien lourdement;
Elle ne demande pas les pompes
Ni l'ornement;
Dedans une chétive étable
Se veut ranger,
Où n'y a ni buffet ni table
Pour y manger."

4. *"Encore faut-il que l'accouchée*
Ait un berceau,
Pour bercer, quand elle est couchée,
L'enfant nouveau:
N'a-t-elle pas garde et servante
Pour la servir?
N'est-elle pas assez puissante
D'y subvenir?"

5. *"L'enfant a pour berceau la crèche*
Pour sommeiller,
Et une botte d'herbe sèche
Pour oreiller;
Elle a pour toute compagnie
Son cher baron,
Elle a un boeuf pour sa mégnie
Et un ânon.

6. *"Tu me dégôutes, ma voisine,*
D'aller plus loin,
Pour voir une femme en gésine
Dessus du foin,
Pour moi qui ne suis que bergère,
Suis beaucoup mieux,
Que non pas cette ménagère
Sous un toit vieux.

7. *"Ne parle pas ainsi, commère,*
Mais par honneur
Crois-moi que c'est la chaste mère
Du vrai Sauveur,
Qui veut ainsi humblement naître
Nous sauvant tous;
Montrant que, bien qu'il soit le maître,
Et humble et doux.

8. *"Exempte-nous, trés chère dame,*
De tout orgueil;
Quand du corps partira notre âme,
Fais-lui accueil,
La présentant, grande princesse,
A ton cher fils,
Pour participer la liesse
Du paradis.

3. "I am afraid that you're mistaken,
Wrong as can be.
This blessed maiden has no splendid,
Rich place to stay.
She lies within a wretched stable,
Dirty and poor;
There is no table for your presents,
Only the floor."

4. "Surely she has a warm, soft cradle
There for the Child?
One has to rock and calm an Infant
So weak and mild.
What sort of guards and servants has she
To give her aid?
Cannot the Heav'nly Father's power
Help the poor maid?"

5. "All they could find to be His cradle,
A manger bed;
Bundles of dry and dusty straw to
Pillow His head.
Joseph, her husband, cares for Mary
Best as he can.
In place of servants, ox and donkey
Are looking on."

6. "Traveling tires me, and this journey
Seems a long way
Only to see a new-born baby
Lying on hay.
Maybe you shepherds find excitement
In this affair;
But I am used to things much better
In which to share."

7. "You must not talk that way, my
neighbor,
Mark what I say:
Upon my honor, this is our Savior
Born on this day.
It is His choice to come so humbly
There in a stall,
Granting His pow'r and grace so gently
To one and all."

8. "O Blessed Mother, free us all from
Arrogant pride.
May we, when life on earth is ended,
Haste to your side.
Daring to hope you will present us
To your dear Son,
And that we'll gain the bliss and joy
Of Paradise won."

Cantique de Noël

O HOLY NIGHT

Cappeau de Roquemaure
Translation: John S. Dwight

Adolph Adam, 1803–1856 [WE]

Andante

1. *Mi - nuit, Chré - tiens, — c'est l'heu - re so - len - nel - le Où l'hom - me*

1. O   ho - ly   night! — the stars are bright-ly shin - ing, It is the

Dieu des - cen-dit jus - qu'à nous,

night of the dear Sav-ior's birth;

Pour ef - fa-

Long lay the

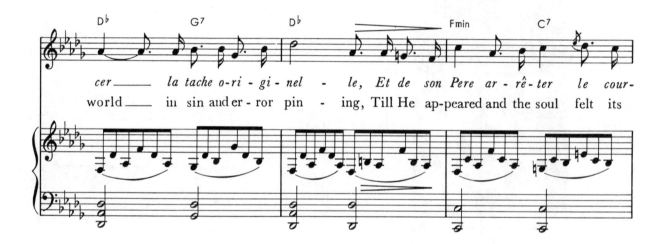

cer _____ la tache o-ri - gi - nel - le, Et de son Pere ar - rê - ter le cour-

world _____ in sin and er-ror pin - ing, Till He ap-peared and the soul felt its

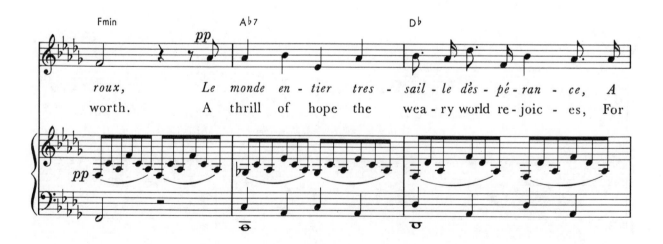

roux, Le monde en - tier tres - sail - le d'es - pé - ran - ce, A

worth. A thrill of hope the wea - ry world re - joic - es, For

cet - te nuit qui lui donne un Sau-veur.___ Peuple à ge-
yon-der breaks a new and glo-rious morn;___ Fall on your

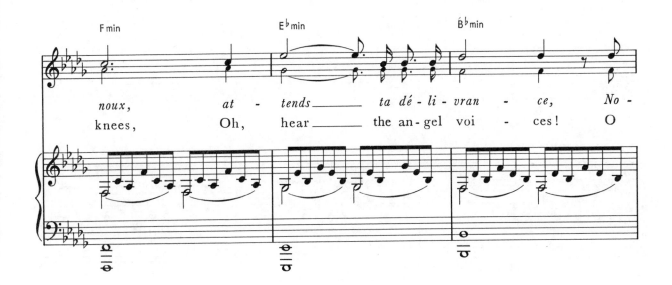

noux, at - tends___ ta dé-li-vran - ce, No -
knees, Oh, hear___ the an-gel voi - ces! O

ël!___ No-ël!___ voi-ci___ le Ré-demp-
night___ di - vine,___ O night___ when Christ was

109

2. *De notre foi que la lumière ardente*
   Nous guide tous au berceau de l'enfant,
   Comme autrefois une étoile brillante
   Y conduisit les chefs de l'Orient.
   Le Roi de rois naît dans une humble
        crèche;
   Puissants du jour, fiers de votre grandeur.
   A votre orgueil c'est de la qu'un Dieu
        prêche.
   Courbez vos fronts devant le Rédempteur!
   Courbez vos fronts devant le Rédempteur!

2. Led by the light of Faith serenely
        beaming,
   With glowing hearts by His cradle we
        stand.
   So, led by light of a star sweetly gleaming,
   Here came the wise men from Orient
        land.
   The King of Kings lay thus in lowly
        manger,
   In all our trials born to be our friend;
   He knows our need, our weakness is no
        stranger;
   Behold your King! Before Him lowly
        bend!
   Behold your King! Before Him lowly
        bend!

3. *Le Rédempteur a brisé toute entrave,*
   La terre est libre et le ciel est ouvert;
   Il voit un frère où n'était qu'un esclave;
   L'amour unit ceux qu'enchaînait le fer
   Qui lui dira notre reconnaissance?
   C'est pour nous tous qu'il nait, qu'il
        souffre et meurt.
   Peuple, debout, chante ta délivrance.
   Noël, Noël, chantons le Rédempteur!
   Noël, Noël, chantons le Rédempteur!

3. Truly He taught us to love one another,
   His law is love, and His gospel is peace;
   Chains shall He break, for the slave is our
        brother,
   And in His name all oppression shall
        cease.
   Sweet hymns of joy in grateful chorus
        raise we,
   Let all within us praise His holy name;
   Christ is the Lord, O praise His name
        forever!
   His pow'r and glory evermore proclaim!
   His pow'r and glory evermore proclaim!

Pat-a-Pan

Bernard de la Monnoye [GKE]

Bernard de la Monnoye, 1700 [WE]

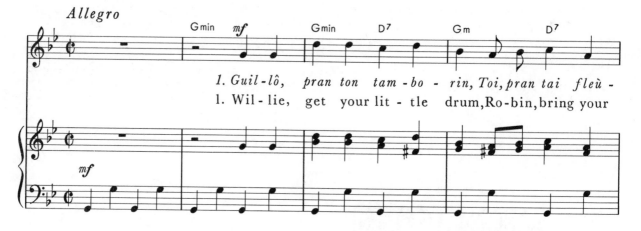

Allegro

Gmin   *mf*   Gmin   D⁷   Gm   D⁷

1. Guil-lô, pran ton tam - bo - rin, Toi, pran tai fleù -
1. Wil - lie, get your lit - tle drum, Ro-bin, bring your

mf

D   C#dim⁷   D   D

te, Ro -   bin; Au son de cés in - stru -
flute, and come. Aren't they fun to play up -

man,　Tu - re - lu - re - lu,　pat - a - pat - a - pan;　Au son
on?　Tu - re - lu - re - lu,　pat - a - pat - a - pan;　When you

de　cés　in - stru - man,　Je di - ron No - ei gai - man.
play your fife and drum, How can an - y - one be glum?

2. C'étò lai môde autrefoi
　De loüé le Roi dé Roi:
　Au son de cés instruman,
　Turelurelu, patapatapan,
　Au son de cés instruman,
　Ai nos an fau faire autan.

3. L'home et Dei son pu d'aicor
　Que lai fleùte et le tambor:
　Au son de cés instruman,
　Turelurelu, patapatapan,
　Au son de cés instruman,
　Chanton, danson, sautons-an!

2. When the men of olden days
　Gave the King of Kings their praise,
　They had pipes to play upon.
　Turelurelu, patapatapan.
　And also the drums they'd play,
　Full of joy, on Christmas Day.

3. God and man today become
　Closely joined as flute and drum.
　Let the joyous tune play on!
　Turelurelu, patapatapan,
　As the instruments you play,
　We will sing, this Christmas day.

BALLADE DE JÉSUS-CHRIST
BALLAD OF JESUS CHRIST

Traditional French [GKE]

Traditional French [WE]

Andante moderato

1. Jé - sus Christ s'ha - bille en___ pau - vre: "Fai - tes - moi la
1. Je - sus came in gar - ment___ low - ly: "Give to me Thy

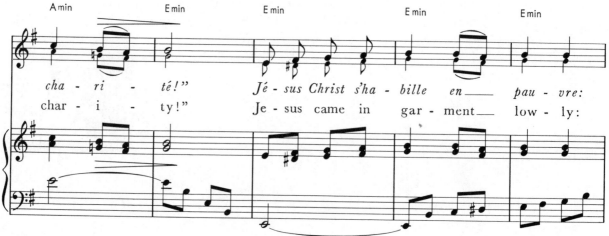

cha - ri - té!" Jé - sus Christ s'ha - bille en___ pau - vre:
char - i - ty!" Je - sus came in gar - ment___ low - ly:

114

"Fai - tes - moi la cha - ri - té! Des miet - tes de vo - tre
"Give to me Thy char - i - ty! On the crumbs that leave thy

ta - ble Je fe - rai bien mon dî - ner."
ta - ble, I shall dine most grate - ful - ly."

2. *"Madame, qu'êtes en fenêtre,*
   Faites-moi la charité!
   Madame, qu'êtes en fenêtre,
   Faites-moi la charité!"
   "Ah! montez, montez, bon pauvre,
   Un bon souper trouverez."

2. "Lady, standing by your window,
   Give to me your charity.
   Lady, standing by your window,
   Give to me your charity."
   "Come in from the cold, my poor One—
   I will find a meal for Thee."

3. *Comme ils montaient le degrés,*
   Trois beaux ang's les éclairaient,
   Comme ils montaient le degrés,
   Trois beaux ang's les éclairaient,
   "Ah! ne craignez rien, Madame,
   "C'est la lune qui paraît."

3. As He softly stepped o'er the threshold,
   Round Him hovered angels bright.
   As He softly stepped o'er the threshold,
   Round Him hovered angels bright.
   "Lady, pray do not be fearful—
   It is but the moon's soft light."

115

QUOIQUE SOYEZ PETIT ENCORE

ALTHOUGH YOU STILL ARE WEAK AND HELPLESS

18th Century French [GKE]

18th Century French Carol [WE]

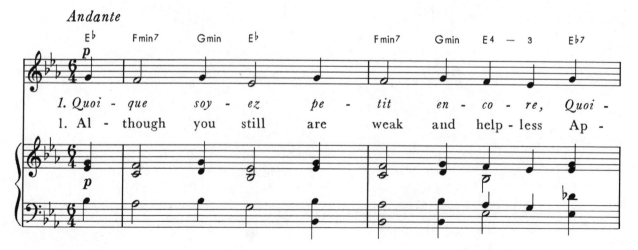

1. Quoi - que soy - ez pe - tit en - co - re, Quoi -
1. Al - though you still are weak and help - less Ap -

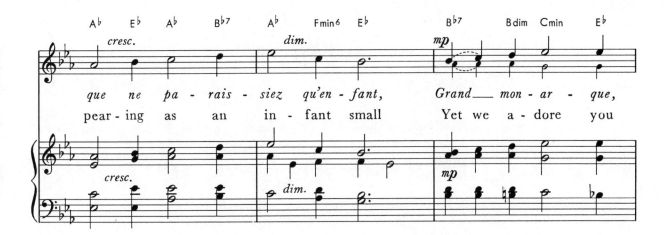

que ne pa - rais - siez qu'en - fant, Grand___ mon - ar - que,

pear - ing as an in - fant small Yet we a - dore you

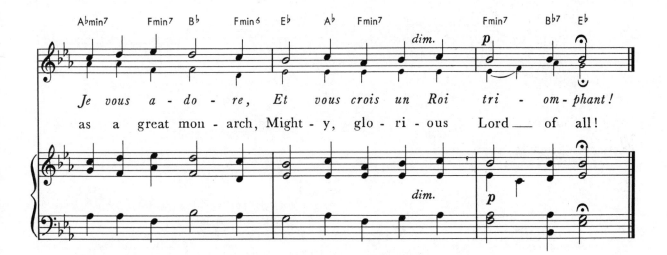

Je vous a - do - re, Et vous crois un Roi tri - om - phant!

as a great mon - arch, Might - y, glo - ri - ous Lord___ of all!

2. Que je découvre de merveilles,
   Quoique petit vous êtes grand;
   Faiblesse et grandeur sans pareilles,
   Vous êtes frêle et tout puissant.

3. Vous n'avons pas en abondance
   De biens pour en faire présent,
   Mais nous donnons a son enfance
   Notr' amour à nous pauvre gens.

4. Dormez, dormez deux ou trois heures,
   Dormez, enfant de l'Éternel!
   Vous retournons à nos demeures
   Après avoir chanté Noël!

2. O, how we marvel at the wonder
   That lies before us, loveliest flow'r!
   Mildness and grandeur past all
      comparing,
   Frailty mingled with greatest pow'r!

3. Though we are poor and humble people,
   That only simple gifts can bring,
   Here are our hearts, and all our devotion,
   Love undying to you, our King.

4. Now may your sleep be sweet and
      peaceful,
   O God, who comes to earth to dwell;
   As to our homes our steps we are turning,
   Praise we sing you: Noel! Noel!

Noël Nouvelet

CHRISTMAS COMES ANEW

Traditional French [GKE]   Traditional French [WE]

Andante con moto

1. No - ël nou - ve - let, No - ël chan - tons i - ci,
1. Christ - mas comes a - new, O let us — sing No - el!

De - vo - tés gens, cri - ons à — Dieu mer - ci!
Glo - ry to God! Now let your — prai - ses swell!

REFRAIN

Chan - tons No - ël pour le Roi nou - ve - let, No - ël!
Sing we No - el for Christ, the new - born King, No - el!

Chan - tons No - ël pour le Roi nou - ve - let, _____
Sing we No - el for Christ, the new - born King. _____

No - ël nou - ve - let, No - ël chan - tons i - ci!
Christ - mas comes a - new, O, let us _ sing No - el!

2. *L'Ange disait! pasteurs partez d'ici!*
   En Bethléem trouverez l'agnelet.
   Refrain

3. *En Bethléem, étant tous réunis,*
   Trouverent l'enfant, Joseph, Marie aussi.
   Refrain

4. *Bientôt, les Rois, par l'étoile eclaircis,*
   A Bethléem vinrent un matinée
   Refrain

5. *L'un partait l'or; l'autre l'encens bém;*
   L'étable alors au Paradis semblait.
   Refrain

2. Angels did say, "O shepherds, come and see,
   Born in Bethlehem, a blessed Lamb for thee."
   Refrain

3. In the manger bed, the shepherds found the Child;
   Joseph was there, and Mother Mary mild.
   Refrain

4. Soon came the kings from following the star,
   Bearing costly gifts from Eastern lands afar.
   Refrain

5. Brought to Him gold and incense of great price;
   Then the stable bare resembled Paradise.
   Refrain

DORS, MA COLOMBE

SLEEP, LITTLE DOVE   (Noël Alsacien)*

Emile Blémont
Translation: E. Cuthbert Nunn, 1868–1914

Traditional Alsatian [WE]

Andante sostenuto

"Dors, ma co - lom - be, Dors, le soir tom - be,"
"Dors, moi je veil - le, Quand on som - meil - le

"Sleep, lit - tle Dove,___ The sky's dark a - bove,"___ The
"My watch I'm keep - ing, While Thou art sleep - ing;

Chan - te la Vierge___ a l'En - fant Dieu.
On voit s'ou - vrir___ le grand ciel bleu."

Vir - gin sang to her in - fant Son;
Swift - ly to Heav - en Thy dreams shall run."

REFRAIN

Chan - tez, beaux an - ges, Ber - cez ___ l'En - fant Qui
Sing, ho - ly an - gels your sweet ___ lull - a - bys,

*The German text for this carol may be found on page 322.

dans ____ ses lang - es, Rit en rê - vant.
Smil - ing and dream - ing my lit - tle One lies.

Chan - tez, beaux an - ges, Ber - cez ___ en ___ choeur Sous
Sing, ho - ly an - gels your sweet ___ lull - a - bys. ___

vos ____ lou - an - ges l'En - fant vain - queur.
Smil - ing and dream - ing my lit - tle One lies.

2. Dors! l'humble étable
   Est charitable
   Et t'offre un nid dont j'ai bien soin.
   La nuit est fraîche,
   Mais dans la crèche
   Comme on a chaud parmi le foin!
       Refrain

2. Humble this stable,
   Hay but the cradle,
   Off'ring a nest of which I've need;
   Chill night's a danger,
   But in the manger
   All in the hay, no cold He'll heed.
       Refrain

Berger, Secoue Ton Sommeil Profond
SHEPHERD, SHAKE OFF YOUR DROWSY SLEEP

Traditional French
Translation: Anonymous

Traditional Besançon Carol
Harmonized by John Stainer [WE]

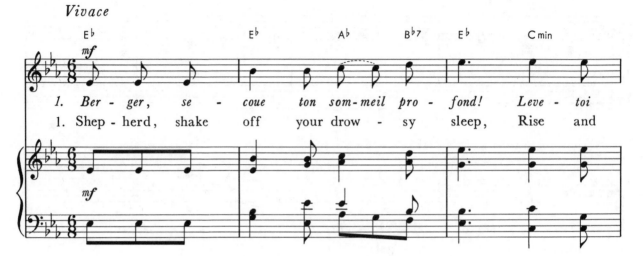

1. Ber - ger, se - coue ton som-meil pro - fond! Leve - toi
1. Shep - herd, shake off your drow - sy sleep, Rise and

et laisse tes mou-tons jou - er; An - ges du Ciel chan - tant très
leave___ your sil - ly sheep; An - gels from Heav'n a - round are

122

fort_____ Ap-por-tez - nous____ la grande____ nou - velle._____

sing - ing, Ti - dings of ____ great joy ____ are bring - ing.

REFRAIN

poco rit.

Ber-ger, en choeur chan-tez No - ël, O, chan-tez No - ël,____ No - ël!

Shep-herd! the cho - rus come and swell! Sing No - el, O sing____ No - el!

poco rit.

2. *Vois comme les fleurs s'ouvrent de
      nouveau,
   Vois que la neige est rosée d'été,
   Vois les étoiles brillent de nouveau,
   Jetant leurs rayons les plus lumineux.*
         Refrain

3. *Berger, levez-vous, hâtez-vous!
   Allez chercher l'Enfant avant le jour.
   Il est l'espoir de chaque nation,
   Tous en Lui trouveront la Rédemption.*
         Refrain

2. See how the flow'rs all burst anew,
   Thinking snow is summer dew;
   See how the stars afresh are glowing,
   All their brightest beams bestowing.
         Refrain

3. Shepherd, then up and quick away!
   Seek the Babe ere break of day.
   He is the hope of ev'ry nation,
   All in Him shall find salvation.
         Refrain

Nöel des Ausels

WHENCE COMES THIS RUSH OF WINGS AFAR ?

Traditional French
Translation: Anonymous

Traditional Bas-Quercy Carol [WE]

Allegretto moderato

1. Ai - ci l'es - te - lo   de   Na - dal
1. Whence comes this rush   of   wings   a - far,

1. Ai - ci l'es - te - lo   de   Na - dal
1. Whence comes this   rush of wings a - far,

Qu'es   a - quel brut   sur   no - stre ous - tal ?
Fol - low-ing straight the   No - el   star ?

Qu'es   a - quel   brut   sur   nos-tre ous - tal ?
Fol - low-ing   straight the   No-el   star ?

124

2. *Dens l'estable ount lou rei del cèl,*
   Dorm entre l'ase et l'ou maurel.
   "Disas, ausèls, que benès fa?"
   "—Benen nostre Dius adoura."

3. *Lou poul s'abanca lou promié,*
   Mounta sul bouès del rastellé,
   Et, per commenca l'ouresou
   Entouna son "coucouroucou."

4. *Lou cardi sourien de soun niu,*
   Saludo e dis: "tirli, chiu, chiu,"
   "Chiu, chiu," respons lou passerat,
   E la calle fa "palpabat."

2. "Tell us, ye birds, why come ye here,
   Into this stable, poor and drear?"
   "Hast'ning we seek the new-born King,
   And all our sweetest music bring."

3. Hark how the Greenfinch bears his part,
   Philomel, too, with tender heart,
   Chants from her leafy dark retreat,
   "Re, mi, fa, sol," in accents sweet.

4. Angels and shepherds, birds of the sky,
   Come where the Son of God doth lie;
   Christ on earth with man doth dwell,
   Join in the shout, "Noel, Noel!"

LA MARCHE DES ROIS

MARCH OF THE KINGS

Traditional French [GKE]

13th Century Provencal Carol [WE]

Allegro moderato

1. Ce ma - tin, j'ai ren - con - tré le train De trois grands Rois qui al - laient
1. This great day, I met up - on the way, The Kings of East as they came

1. Ce ma - tin, J'ai ren - con - tré le train De trois grands
1. This great day, I met up - on the way, The Kings of

en voy - a - ge,— Ce ma - tin, J'ai ren - con - tré le train, De
ri - ding proud - ly,—This great day, I met up - on the way, The

Rois qui al - laient en voy - a - ge,—Ce ma - tin, J'ai ren - con - tré le
East as they come ri - ding proud - ly, This great day, I met up - on the

trois grands Rois des-sus le grand che-min. Tout char-gés d'or les sui-
Kings of East with all their fine ar-ray. The gifts of gold, frank-in-

train des-sus le grand che-min.
Kings with all their fine ar-ray.

vant d'a-bord, De grands guer-riers et les gar-des du tré-sor, Tout
cense, and myrrh Were guard-ed close by a band of sturd-y war-riors, Their

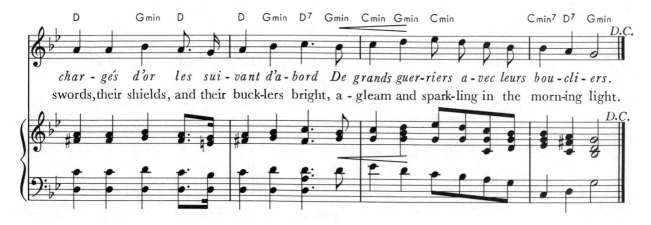

char-gés d'or les sui-vant d'a-bord De grands guer-riers a-vec leurs bou-cli-ers.
swords, their shields, and their buck-lers bright, a - gleam and spark-ling in the morn-ing light.

Un Flambeau, Jeannette, Isabelle

BRING A TORCH, JEANNETTE, ISABELLA

Traditional Provençal, 17th Century
Translation: E. Cuthbert Nunn, 1868–1914

17th Century Provençal Carol [WE]

1. Un flam - beau,___ Jean - nette, Is - a - bel - le,
1. Bring a torch,___ Jean - nette, Is - a - bel - la,

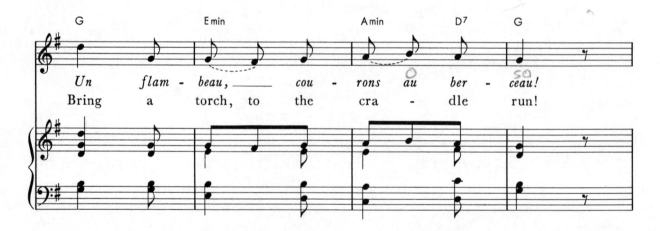

Un flam - beau,___ cou - rons au ber - ceau!
Bring a torch, to the cra - dle run!

C'est Jé - sus, bon - nes gens du ha - meau,___ Le Christ est
It is Je - sus, good folk of the vil - lage; Christ___ is

2. C'est un tort quand l'Enfant sommeille,
   C'est un tort de crier si fort.
   Taisez-vous, l'un et l'autre, d'abord!
   Au moindre bruit, Jésus s'eveille,
   Chut! chut! chut! Il dort à merveille,
   Chut! chut! chut! voyez comme Il dort!

3. Doucement, dans l'étable close,
   Doucement, venez un moment!
   Approchez, que Jésus est charmant!
   Comme Il est blanc, comme Il est rose!
   Do! do! do! que l'Enfant repose!
   Do! do! do! qu'Il rit en dormant!

2. It is wrong when the Child is sleeping,
   It is wrong to talk so loud;
   Silence, all, as you gather around,
   Lest your noise should waken Jesus:
   Hush! hush! see how fast He slumbers;
   Hush! hush! see how fast He sleeps!

3. Softly to the little stable,
   Softly for a moment come;
   Look and see how charming is Jesus,
   How He is white, His cheeks are rosy!
   Hush! hush! see how the Child is sleeping;
   Hush! hush! see how He smiles in dreams.

Touro-Louro-Louro

Traditional Provençal Carol [GKE]   Nicolas Saboly, 1614–1675 [WE]

Allegretto

1. *Tou - ro - lou - ro - lou - ro! lou gau can - to, E n'es*
1. Tou - ro - lou - ro - lou - ro, cocks are crow - ing, Long be -

pas in - ca - ro jour; Iéu m'en vau en Ter - ro
fore the morn - ing light, High a - bove, the stars are

San - to Pèr vè ire No - ste Se - gnour. Vo - stu vé -
glow - ing, O'er the Ho - ly Land to - night. "Will you go

130

131

fa - rai iéu? Siéu pa-vou rous coume un__ pou-
I must go; Though the ___ jour-ney will __ be

let Quand siéu sou - let, Quand siéu __ sou - let.
long, Still I must go, Yea, I __ must go.

2. Touro-louro-louro! l'auro méno
   E mé fai boufa lei det;
   Certes iéu siéu bèn en péno,
   Ai póu dé mouri dé fré;
   Hóu dé l'oustau!
   Qui pico avau?
   Voudriéu lóuja.
   Sian tous couija!
   Granjièro! Granjièro!
   Durbèsmé siéu tout jala;
   Boutasmé dins la fénièro!
   Hélas, moun Diéu!
   Que ferai iéu?
   Lour paure! rounte tirarai?
   Beléu mourrai, Beléu mourrai.

2. Touro-louro-louro, colds winds blowing
   Make my body numb with cold;
   But I cannot yet be stopping,
   For the day is growing old.
   "Please let me rest."
   "No rest for you."
   "I must find rest."
   "No rest for you."
   O farmer, O farmer,
   Give me shelter for the night,
   In the hay-loft I'd be sleeping.
   Some shelter, pray,
   Just for this day,
   For I'm near to freezing now.
   Don't let me die! Don't let me die!

3. Touro-louro-louro! pèr fourtuno
   Siéu sourti d'un michant pas;
   La pode coumta pèr uno!
   Enfin ai trouba lou jas.
   Bonjour à tous!
   Amai à vous.
   E qué fasès?
   Vous lou vésès.
   Mario! Mario!
   Vous estrugué d'un bèu friéu,
   Lou veritable Messio!
   Bon Sant Jóusè,
   Sé mé crésè.
   Mé faré vèire aquel enfant
   Qu'iéu ame tan, Qu'iéu ame tan.

3. Touro-louro-louro, what good fortune,
   I have found the Holy Child!
   There upon the straw, the handsome
   Baby looks at me and smiles!
   "Good day to you!"
   (He's laughing now!)
   "Good day to you!"
   (Joseph's so proud!)
   O Mary, O Mary,
   May your name be ever blest
   For the Babe that Heaven sent thee!
   Saint Joseph, too,
   Blessings on you!
   For the lovely Child so dear
   That we all love, That we all love.

D'où Viens-Tu, Bergère?

WHENCE ART THOU, MY MAIDEN?

Traditional French Canadian
Translation: William McLennan, 1866

Traditional French Canadian [WE]

1. "D'où viens-tu, ber-gè-re, d'où viens-tu?"
1. "Whence art thou, my mai-den, whence art thou?"

"Je viens de l'é-tab-le, de m'y pro-me-ner,____
"I come from the sta-ble where, this ver-y night,____

133

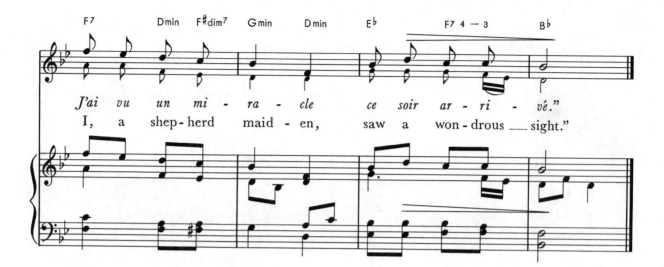

J'ai vu un mi - ra - cle ce soir ar - ri - vé."
I, a shep - herd maid - en, saw a won - drous ___ sight."

2. "Qu'as-tu vu, bergère, qu'as tu vu?
   Qu'as-tu vu, bergère, qu'as tu vu?"
   "J'ai vu dans la crèche un petit enfant
   Sur la paille fraîche, mis bien tendre-
   ment."

2. "What saw'st thou, my maiden, what
   saw'st thou?
   What saw'st thou, my maiden, what saw'st
   thou?"
   "There within a manger, a little Child I
   saw
   Lying, softly sleeping, on a bed of straw."

3. "Rien de plus, bergère, rien de plus?
   Rien de plus, bergère, rien de plus?"
   "Saint' Marie, sa mère, qui lui fait boir'
   du lait,
   Saint Joseph, son père, qui tremble de
   froid."

3. "Nothing more, my maiden, nothing
   more?
   Nothing more, my maiden, nothing
   more?"
   "There I saw the mother her sweet Baby
   hold,
   And the father, Joseph, trembling with
   the cold."

4. "Rien de plus, bergère, rien de plus?
   Rien de plus, bergère, rien de plus?
   "Y-a le boeuf et l'âne, qui sont par devant
   Avec leur haleine rechauffant l'enfant."

4. "Nothing more, my maiden, nothing
   more?
   Nothing more, my maiden, nothing
   more?"
   "I saw ass and oxen, kneeling meek and
   mild,
   With their gentle breathing warm the holy
   Child."

5. "Rien de plus, bergère, rien de plus?
   Rien de plus, bergère, rien de plus?"
   "Y-a trois petits anges descendus du ciel,
   Chantant les louanges du Père éternel."

5. "Nothing more, my maiden, nothing
   more?
   Nothing more, my maiden, nothing
   more?"
   "There were three bright angels come
   down from the sky,
   Singing forth sweet praises to our God on
   high."

134

GERMAN CAROLS

O Du Fröhliche
O HOW JOYFULLY

Johannes Falk, 1816 [GKE]

From Latin Hymn, "O Sanctissima" [WE]

Andante sostenuto
REFRAIN

1. O du fröh - li - che, —— O du se - li - ge, ——
1. O how joy - ful - ly, —— O how bless - ed - ly, ——

gna - den - brin - gen - de Weih - nachts - zeit!
Comes the glo - ry of Christ - mas - time!

136

VERSE

Welt___ ging ver - lo - ren, Christ___ ist ge - bo - ren:
To a world so lost in sin, Christ the Sav - ior, en - ters in:

Freu - e,___ freu - e dich, O Chri - sten - heit!
Praise Him, all ye Christ - ians, praise Him ev - er - more!

2. *Christ ist erschienen,*
   Uns zu versühnen:
   Freue, freue dich, O Christenheit!

2. Jesus, born in lowly stall
   With His grace redeems us all:
   Praise Him, all ye Christians, praise Him
   evermore!

3. *Himmlische Heere*
   Jauchzen dir Ehre:
   Freue, freue dich, O Christenheit!

3. Hosts of angels from on high.
   Sing, rejoicing, in the sky:
   Praise Him, all ye Christians, praise Him
   evermore!

O Tannenbaum

O CHRISTMAS TREE

Traditional German [GKE]

Traditional German [WE]

Tan - nen-baum, Wie treu sind dei - ne Blät - ter!
Christ-mas tree, With faith-ful leaves un - chang - ing.

2. *O Tannenbaum, O Tannenbaum,*
   Du kannst mir sehr gefallen!
   Wie oft hat mich zur Weihnachtszeit
   Ein Baum von dir mich hoch erfreut!
   O Tannenbaum, O Tannenbaum,
   Du kannst mir sehr gefallen!

3. *O Tannenbaum, O Tannenbaum,*
   Dein Kleid soll mich was lehren!
   Die Hoffnung und Beständigkeit
   Gibt Trost und Kraft zu aller Zeit.
   O Tannenbaum, O Tannenbaum,
   Dein Kleid soll mich was lehren!

2. O Christmas tree, O Christmas tree,
   Of all the trees most lovely;
   Each year, you bring to me delight
   Gleaming in the Christmas night.
   O Christmas tree, O Christmas tree,
   Of all the trees most lovely.

3. O Christmas tree, O Christmas tree,
   Your leaves will teach me, also,
   That hope and love and faithfulness
   Are precious things I can possess.
   O Christmas tree, O Christmas tree,
   Your leaves will teach me, also.

139

KLING, GLÖCKCHEN
RING, LITTLE BELLS

Karl Enslin, 1814–1875 [GKE]

Traditional German Carol [WE]

Allegro ma non troppo

1. Kling, Glöck-chen, klin-ge-lin-ge-ling, Kling, Glöck-chen, kling!
1. Ring, bells, go ting-a-ling-a-ling, Ring, lit-tle bells!

Laßt mich ein, ihr Kin-der, Ist so kalt der Win-ter,
O how cold the win-ter! Will you let Me en-ter?

Öff - net mir die Tü - ren, Laßt mich nicht er - frie - ren.
Do not bar the door - way On my bless - ed birth - day!

Kling, Glöck-chen, klin-ge-lin-ge-ling, Kling, glöck-chen, kling!
Ring, bells, go ting-a-ling-a-ling, Ring, lit-tle bells!

2. *Kling, Glöckchen, klingelingeling,*
   Kling, Glöckchen, kling!
   Mädchen hört und Bübchen,
   Macht mir auf das Stübchen,
   Bring euch viele Gaben,
   Sollt euch dran erlaben.
   Kling, Glöckchen, klingelingeling,
   Kling, Glöckchen, kling!

2. Ring, bells, go tingalingaling,
   Ring, little bells!
   Maid and Infant tender,
   Will you let Us enter?
   To Us shelter giving,
   And the Father praising?
   Ring, bells, go tingalingaling,
   Ring, little bells!

3. *Kling, Glöckchen, kingelingeling,*
   Kling, Glöckchen, kling!
   Hell erglühn die Kerzen,
   Öffnet mir die Herzen!
   Will drin wohnen fröhlich,
   Frommes Kind, wie selig!
   Kling, Glöckchen, klingelingeling,
   Kling, Glöckchen, kling!

3. Ring, bells, go tingalingaling,
   Ring, little bells!
   In our hearts now stealing,
   'Mid the bells all pealing,
   Joy and blessing holy
   From the Child so lowly,
   Ring, bells, go tingalingaling,
   Ring, little bells!

Ihr Kinderlein, Kommet

O COME, LITTLE CHILDREN

Christoph von Schmid, 1768–1854 [GKE]

J.A.P. Schulz, 1747–1800 [WE]

Moderato

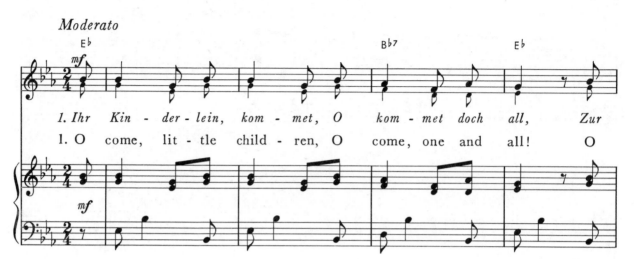

1. Ihr Kin - der - lein, kom - met, O kom - met doch all, Zur
1. O come, lit - tle child - ren, O come, one and all! O

Krip - pe her kom - met in Beth - le - hem's Stall Und
come to the cra - dle in Beth - le - hem's stall! Come,

seht, was in die - ser hoch - hei - li - gen Nacht Der
see what has hap - pened this ho - li - est night; Come,

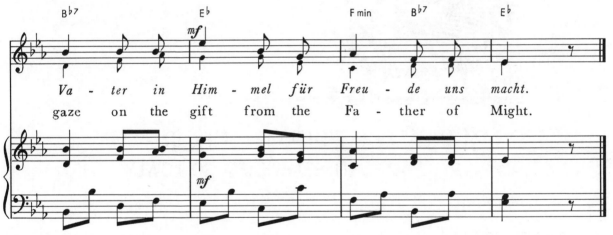

Va - ter in Him - mel für Freu - de uns macht.
gaze on the gift from the Fa - ther of Might.

2. *Da liegt es, ihr Kinder, auf Heu und auf Stroh,*
Maria und Joseph betrachten es froh,
Der edlichen Hirten knie'n betend davor,
Hoch oben schwebt jubelnd der Engelein Chor.

3. *O beugt, wie die Hirten, anbetend die Knie,*
Erhebet die Händlein und danket wie sie!
Stimmt freudig, ihr Kinder, wer sollt' ich nicht freu'n?
Stimmt freudig zum Jubel der Engel mit ein.

2. How sweetly He lies in His bed made of straw,
As Mary and Joseph behold Him in awe!
The shepherds are kneeling before His poor bed,
While caroling angels are heard overhead.

3. O come, join the shepherds, and on bended knee
Give thanks to the Father for Jesus, our King.
O lift up your voices and join in the praise,
That angels from Heav'n to the Father now raise.

ZU BETHLEHEM GEBOREN
IN BETHLEHEM SO LOWLY

Traditional German [GKE]

Geistliche Psalter, 1638 [WE]

1. Zu Beth - le - hem ge - bo - ren Ist uns ein Kind - e - lein Das

1. In Beth - le - hem so low - ly, There came to earth for me A

144

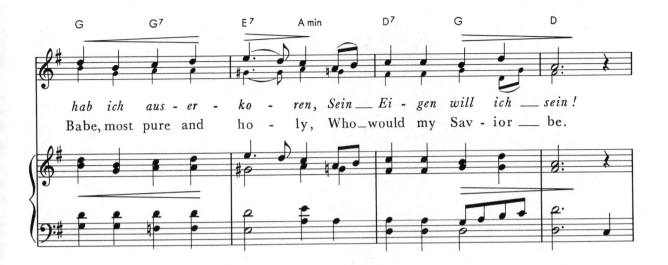

hab ich aus - er - ko - ren, Sein __ Ei - gen will ich __ sein!
Babe, most pure and ho - ly, Who __ would my Sav - ior __ be.

E - ia, E - ia,
E - ia, E - ia,
E - ia, E - ia, Sein __ Ei - gen __ will ich sein.
E - ia, E - ia, Who __ would my __ Sav - ior be.

2. *Aus ganzem, reinem Herzen*
   Will ich dich lieben, Herr,
   In Freuden und in Schmerzen,
   Je länger und je mehr.
   Eia, eia,
   Je länger und je mehr.

2. Dear Babe, I'll always love Thee
   Whatever is in store.
   In joy and pain I'll serve Thee,
   Now and forevermore.
   Eia, eia,
   Now and forevermore.

ALS ICH BEI MEINEN SCHAFEN WACHT

WHILE BY MY SHEEP (Echo Carol)

Traditional German
Translation: Theodore Baker

Trier Gesangbuch, 1871 [WE]

2. *Er sagt es soll geboren sein*
   Zu Bethlehem ein Kindelein.
   Refrain

3. *Er sagt das Kind lag da im Stall*
   Und sollt die Welt erlösen all.
   Refrain

4. *Den Schatz muss ich bewahren wohl,*
   So bleibt mein Herz der Freude voll.
   Refrain

2. There shall be born, so he did say,
   In Bethlehem, a Child today.
   Refrain

3. There shall He lie, in manger mean,
   Who shall redeem the world from sin.
   Refrain

4. Lord, evermore to me be nigh,
   Then shall my heart be filled with joy!
   Refrain

Josef, Lieber Josef Mein

JOSEPH, DEAREST JOSEPH MINE

Traditional German [GKE]　　　　　　　　　　　　　　　14th Century German [WE]

1. "Jo - sef, lie - ber Jo - sef mein, Hilf mir wie - gen das
1. Jo - seph, dear - est Jo - seph mine, Help me rock the

Kin - de - lein, Will es wie - gen und sing - en ein: 'Nun
Child di - vine, Sing to Him a lull - a - bye: 'Now

schlaf in ruh, dein Äug - lein zu, O Je - su!' "
sleep and rest, Your slum - ber blest, O Je - sus!' "

148

REFRAIN

Er ist er-schie-nen am heu-ti-gen Tag, Am heu-ti-gen Tag in Is-ra-el,
He came a-mong us at Christ-mas time, At Christ-mas time in Beth-le-hem,

Der Ma-ri-a ver-kün-digt ist durch Ga-bri-el. Ei - a,
Bring-ing all — men far and wide Love's Di-a-dem. Ei - a,

e - ia, Je-sum Christ hat uns ge-born Ma-ri - a.
e - ia, Je-sus Christ, who came to earth to save us.

2. *"Gerne, liebe Mädel mein,*
   Will ich wiege das Kindelein,
   Will es wiegen und singen ein:
   'Nun schlaf in Ruh, die Äuglein zu, O
   Jesu.'"
        Refrain

2. "Gladly, Mother Mary mine,
   Will I rock the Child divine,
   While I sing a lullaby:
   'O sleep and rest, Your slumber blest,
   Dear Jesus.'"
        Refrain

Am Weihnachtsbaum die Lichter Brennen

THE CHRISTMAS TREE WITH ITS CANDLES GLEAMING

Traditional German [GKE]   Traditional German [WE]

Andante

1. Am Weih - nachts - baum _____ die Licht - er bren - nen, Wie glänzt er

1. The Christ - mas tree, with its can - dles gleam - ing, A glow is

fest - lich,___ lieb und __ mild, Als spräch er: "Wollt___ in mir er-

kind - ling in all our __ hearts. It speaks of God's __ pure love-light

ken - nen, Ge - treu - er Hoff - nung still - es___ Bild."

stream - ing; It brings us hope, and joy im - parts.

2. *Die Kinder stehn mit hellen Blicken,*
   Das Auge lacht, es lacht das Herz.
   O fröhlich, seliges Entzücken!
   Die Alten schauen himmelwärts.

2. The children stand round the glitt'ring treasure,
   Their eyes are sparkling, their spirits bright.
   O sweet reminder of love's full measure,
   Our shining symbol of heav'nly light!

3. *Gesegnet seid ihr alten Leute,*
   Gesegnet sei du kleine Schar!
   Wir bringen Gottes Segen heute
   Dem braunen, wie dem weissen Haar.

3. For ev'ry heart, you offer blessing,
   For ev'ry parent as well as child;
   For young and old, your beacons beck'ning
   Lead us to Jesus, sweet and mild.

Susani

14th Century German Carol [GKE]

Cologne, 1623 [WE]

1. Vom him - mel hoch, O Eng - lein, kommt!
1. From Heav'n on high, O an - gels, sing!

Ei - a! ei - a! Su - sa - ni,
Ei - a! ei - a! Su - sa - ni,

su - sa - ni, su - sa - ni! Kommt, singt und klingt, kommt
su - sa - ni, su - sa - ni! And let the joy - ful

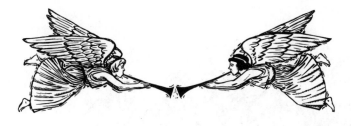

pfeift___ und trombt! Al - le - lu - ja! Al - le - lu -
trum - pets ring! Al - le - lu - ja! Al - le - lu -

ja! Von Je - sus singt___ und Ma - ri - a.
ja! Of Ma - ry sing,___ and Christ, her Son.

2. *Kommt ohne Instrumenten nit!*
   Eia, eia! Susani, susani, susani!
   Bringt Lauten, Harfen, Geigen mit!
   Alleluja! Alleluja!
   Von Jesus singt und Maria!

3. *Lasst hören euer Stimmen viel!*
   Eia, eia! Susani, susani, susani!
   Mit Orgel und mit Saitenspiel!
   Alleluja! Alleluja!
   Von Jesus singt und Maria!

4. *Singt Fried' den Menschen weit und breit!*
   Eia, eia, Susani, susani, susani!
   Gott Preis und Ehr in Ewigkeit!
   Alleluja! Alleluja!
   Von Jesus singt und Maria!

2. Come, bring your instruments so sweet!
   Eia, eia! Susani, susani, susani!
   With harp and chimes your Savior greet!
   Alleluja! Alleluja!
   Of Mary sing, and Christ, her Son!

3. O lift your voices clear and high!
   Eia, eia! Susani, susani, susani!
   With strings and organ raise the cry!
   Alleluja! Alleluja!
   Of Mary sing, and Christ, her Son!

4. Sing Peace to all men far and wide!
   Eia, eia! Susani, susani, susani!
   And praise to God, our heav'nly Guide!
   Alleluja! Alleluja!
   Of Mary sing, and Christ, her Son!

O Laufet, Ihr Hirten
COME RUNNING, YOU SHEPHERDS

Traditional German [GKE]

Traditional Silesian Carol [WE]

Allegretto

1. O lau - fet ihr Hir - ten, lauft al - le zu - gleich, Und
1. Come run - ning, you shep - herds, as fast — as you can, With

neh - men Schal - mei - en und Pfeif - en mit euch! Lauft —
flutes and with bag - pipes, and with — your whole clan. We're —

al - le — zu - mal mit — freu - di - gem — Schall, Nach
go - ing — to — see, In — Beth - le - hem's — stall, The

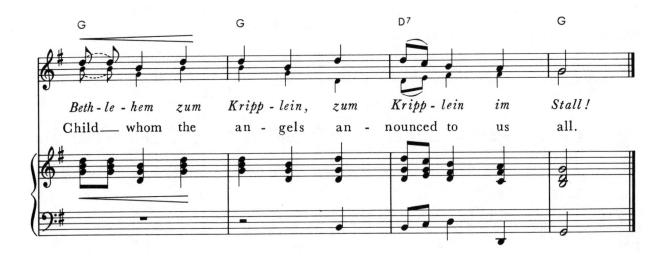

Beth - le - hem zum Kripp - lein, zum Kripp - lein im Stall!
Child — whom the an - gels an - nounced to us all.

2. *Ein Kindlein ist geboren, wie ein Engel
   so schön!*
   Dabei auch sein herzlieber Vater tut stehn.
   *Ein' Jungfrau, schön zart nach englischer
   Art:*
   Es hat mich erbarmet ganz inniglich hart.

3. *Mein Nachbar, lauf hurtig, bring's
   Wieglein daher!*
   *Will Kindlein drein legen, es frieret so
   sehr.*
   Ei, eia popei, lieb's Kindel, schlaf ein
   Im Kripplein, zart's Jesulein, eia popei!

2. This beautiful Infant puts angels to
   shame!
   Beside, Him, shy Joseph is breathing His
   name.
   And Mary is there—so sweet, but so pale!
   My heart fills with pity to see her so frail.

3. My neighbors, we're making a cradle for
   Him,
   To tuck Him in snug from the night, cold
   and grim.
   Loo, loo, lovely Babe; loo, loo—go to sleep.
   O dear little Jesus, loo, loo—go to sleep.

WIEGENLIED DER HIRTEN
SHEPHERDS' CRADLE SONG

C.D. Schubart, 1791 [GKE]

Glatz Folk Song [WE]

Andante cantabile

1. Schlaf wohl, du Him-mels - kna - be du, Schlaf wohl, du sü - ßes Kind,— Dich
1. Sleep well, Thou love - ly heav'n-ly Babe, Sleep well, Thou sweet-est Child,— While

fa - cheln En - ge - lein in Ruh Mit sanf - ten Him - mels - wind.— Wir
an - gels with— their soft white wings Stir bree - zes, cool— and mild.— We

ar - men Hir - ten sin - gen dir Ein herz - ig's Wie - gen - lied - lein für:
shep - herds poor will sing to Thee A lull - a - by,— so ten - der - ly:

Schla - fe,___ schla - fe,___ Him - mels-sohn - chen, schla - fe!
Sleep,_sleep,___ sleep,_sleep,___ Lit - tle Son___ of Heav - en, sleep!

2. *Maria hat mit Mutterlieb*
   Dich leise zugedeckt,
   Und Joseph hält den Hauch zurück,
   Dass er dich nicht erweckt.
   Die Schäflein, die in Stalle sind,
   Verstummen vor dir Himmelskind.
   Schlafe, schlafe,
   Himmels-söhnchen, schlafe!

2. Sleep well while Mary holds Thee close,
   Sleep well upon her breast,
   Dear Joseph scarcely dares to breathe—
   He'd not disturb Thy rest!
   The lambs stand mute about the stall
   As they adore Thee, Lord of All!
   Sleep, sleep,
   Little Son of Heaven, sleep!

LIEB NACHTIGALL, WACH AUF

DEAR NIGHTINGALE, AWAKE

Franconian Folk Carol [GKE]

Bamberger Gesangbuch, 1670 [WE]

Allegretto

1. Lieb Nach - ti - gall, wach auf! Wach auf, du schö - nes Vö - gel - ein Auf
1. Dear Night-in-gale, a - wake! And from the boughs of ev -'ry tree, Come

dei - nem grü - nen Zwei - ge - lein, Wach hur - tig auf, wach auf! Dem
trill the news most joy - ful - ly, A - wake, dear bird, a - wake! Our

Kin - de - lein Aus - er - kor - en, heut ge - bo - ren, fast er - fror - en,
Lord is ___ born! Here from Heav - en is sal - va - tion to us giv - en,

Sing, sing, ___ sing Dem zar - ten ___ Je - su - lein.
Sing, sing, ___ sing To hail ___ the ___ new ___ born ___ King.

2. *Flieg her zum Krippelein!*
   Flieg her, du kleines Schwesterlein,
   Blas an dem feinen Psalterlein,
   Sing, Nachtigall, gar fein.
   Dem Kindelein
   Musiziere, koloriere, jubiliere,
   Sing, sing, sing
   Dem süssen Jesulein

2. To His poor bed now fly,
   My little sister, with your song,
   Amuse the Baby all day long,
   O do not let Him cry!
   In finest tones
   Music bringing, anthems singing, carols
     ringing,
   Sing, sing, sing
   To please the new-born King.

3. *Sing, Nachtigall, ohn' end,*
   Zu vielen hunderttausendmal,
   Das Kindlein lobe ohne Zahl,
   In deine Liebe send!
   Dem Heiland mein
   Ehr beweise, lob und preise, laut und leise,
   Sing, sing, sing
   Dem Christuskindelein!

3. Sing on and on and on;
   A hundred times a thousand ways
   Seek there the precious Babe to praise,
   Till all His fears are gone.
   Our Savior's here!
   Honor showing, rapture glowing, love
     o'erflowing,
   Sing, sing, sing
   To praise the new-born King.

Maria durch ein' Dornwald Ging
MARIA WANDERS THROUGH THE THORN

Traditional German [GKE]

German Medieval Carol
Late 15th or early 16th Century [WE]

2. *Da hab'n die Dornen Rosen getrag'n*
   Kyrie eleison.
   Als das Kindlein durch den Wald
      getrag'n
   Da hab'n die Dornen Rosen getrag'n
   Jesus und Maria.

2. As with the Child she passes near,
   Kyrie eleison.
   As with the Child she passes near,
   Red roses on the thorn appear.
   Jesus and Maria.

VOM HIMMEL HOCH, DA KOMM' ICH HER

FROM HEAVEN ABOVE TO EARTH I COME

Martin Luther, 1535
Translation: Catherine Winkworth, 1829–1878

Melody Published by Leipzig, 1539
(Attributed to Martin Luther)
Harmonization J.S. Bach, 1685–1750

Andante

1. Vom Him-mel hoch da komm' ich her, Ich bring' euch gu-te neu-e Mär, Der gu-ten Mär bring' ich so viel, Da-von ich sing'n und sa-gen will.

1. From heav'n a-bove to earth I come, To bear good news to ev'ry home, Glad ti-dings of great joy I bring, Where-of I now will glad-ly sing.

2. *Euch ist ein Kindlein heut gebor'n,*
   Von einer Jungfrau auserkor'n
   Ein Kindelein so zart und fein,
   Das soll eu'r Freud' und Wonne sein.

2. To you this night is born a Child
   Of Mary, chosen mother mild;
   This little Child, of lowly birth,
   Shall be the joy of all the earth.

3. *Lob, Ehr' sei Gott im höchsten Thron,*
   Der uns schenkt seinen ein'gen Sohn,
   Des freuen sich der Engel Schar
   Und singen uns solch neues Jahr.

3. Glory to God in highest heav'n,
   Who unto us his Son hath giv'n!
   While angels sing with pious mirth,
   A glad New Year to all the earth.

Brich An, Du Schönes Morgenlicht
BREAK FORTH, O BEAUTEOUS HEAVENLY LIGHT

Johann Rist, 1607–1667
Translation: J. Troutbeck, 1832–1899

Johann Schop, died ca 1664
Adapted and Harmonized by J.S. Bach

1. Brich an, du schö-nes Mor-gen-licht, Und lass den Him-mel ta-gen; Du Hir-ten-volk er-stau-ne nicht, Weil dir die En-gel sa-gen, Daß die-ses schwa-che Knä-be-lein Soll un-ser Trost und Freu-de sein, Da-zu den Sa-tan zwin-gen, Und al-les wie-der bring-en.

1. Break forth, O beau-teous heav'n-ly light, And ush-er in the morn-ing; Ye shep-herds, shrink not with af-fright, But hear the an-gel's warn-ing. This Child, now weak in in-fan-cy, Our con-fi-dence and joy shall be, The pow'r of Sa-tan break-ing, Our peace e-ter-nal mak-ing.

162

Ich Steh' an Deiner Krippe Hier
BESIDE THY CRADLE HERE I STAND

Paul Gerhardt, 1607–1676
Translation: J. Troutbeck, 1832–1899

Geistliche Gesangbuch
Harmonized by J.S. Bach

Andante

1. Ich steh' an deiner Krip-pe hier, O Je-su-lein, mein le-ben.
   Ich steh-e, bring' und schen-ke dir Was du mir hast ge-ge-ben.

1. Be-side Thy cra-dle here I stand, O Thou that ev-er liv-est,
   And bring Thee with a will-ing hand The ver-y gifts Thou giv-est.

Nimm hin, es ist mein Geist und Sinn, Herz, Seel' und Mut, nimm'
Ac-cept me, 'tis my mind and heart, My soul, my strength, my

Al-les hin, Und lass dir's wohl-ge-fal-len!
ev-'ry part That Thou from me re-quir-est.

163

Wie Schön Leuchtet der Morgenstern

HOW BRIGHTLY SHINES THE MORNING STAR

Philip Nicolai, 1598
Translation: William Mercer, 1859

Philip Nicolai, 1598
Arranged by J.S. Bach, ca 1730

Reich und Ga - ben. Hoch und sehr präch - tig er - hab - en.
Draw Thou near us; Great Em-man-uel, come and hear us.

2. Ei, meine Perl, du werte Kron,
   Wahr' Gottes und Mariensohn,
   Ein hochgeborner König!
   Mein Herz heisst dich ein Himmelsblum;
   Dein süsses Evangelium
   Ist lauter Milch und Honig.
   Jesu! Jesu!
   Hosianna! Himmlisch' Manna, das wir
      essen,
   Deiner kann ich nicht vergessen.

3. Herr Gott Vater, mein starker Held,
   Du hast mich ewig vor der Welt
   In deinem Sohn geliebet.
   Dein Sohn hat mich ihm selbst vertraut,
   Er ist mein Freund, ich seine Braut,
   Drum mich auch nichts betrübet.
   Eia, eia,
   Himmlisch Leben wird er geben mir dort
      oben:
   Ewig soll mein Herz ihn loben.

2. Though circled by the hosts on high,
   He deigned to cast a pitying eye
   Upon His helpless creature;
   The whole creation's Head and Lord,
   By highest seraphim adored,
   Assumed our very nature;
   Jesus, grant us,
   Through thy merit, to inherit Thy
      salvation.
   Hear, O hear our supplication.

3. Rejoice, ye heav'ns; thou Earth, reply.
   With praise, ye sinners, fill the sky,
   For this, His Incarnation.
   Incarnate God, put forth Thy pow'r,
   Ride on, ride on, great Conqueror,
   Till all know Thy salvation.
   Amen, amen!
   Alleluia! Alleluia! praise be given
   Evermore, by earth and Heaven.

Es Ist ein' Ros' Entsprungen
LO, HOW A ROSE E'ER BLOOMING

Traditional German
Translation: Theodore Baker, 1894

Kölner Gesangbuch, 1599
Harmonization: Michael Praetorius, 1609 [WE]

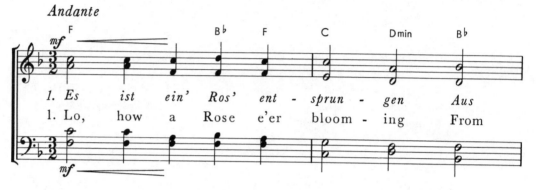

1. Es ist ein' Ros' ent-sprun-gen Aus
1. Lo, how a Rose e'er bloom-ing From

ei-ner Wur-zel zart, Wie uns die Al-ten
ten-der stem hath sprung! Of Jes-se's lin-eage

sun-gen, Aus Jes-se kam die Art, Und
com-ing, As men of old have sung. It

hat ein Blüm-lein bracht___ Mit-ten im kal-ten
came, a flow-'ret bright,___ A-mid the cold of

Win-ter, Wohl zu der___ hal-ben Nacht.
win-ter, When half-spent___ was___ the night.

2. *Das Röslein, das ich meine,*
   Davon Isaias sagt,
   Hat uns gebracht alleine
   Marie, die reine Magd.
   Aus Gottes ew'gem Rat
   Hat sie ein Kind geboren,
   Wohl zu der halben Nacht.

3. *Das Blümelein, so kleine,*
   Das duftet uns so süss;
   Mit seinem hellen Scheine
   Vertreibt's die Finsternis;
   Wahr' Mensch un wahrer Gott,
   Hilft uns aus allen Leiden,
   Rettet von Sünd' und Tod.

2. Isaiah 'twas foretold it,
   The Rose I have in mind,
   With Mary we behold it,
   The Virgin Mother kind.
   To show God's love aright,
   She bore to men a Savior
   When half-spent was the night.

3. This Flow'r, whose fragrance tender
   With sweetness fills the air,
   Dispels with glorious splendor
   The darkness ev'rywhere.
   True man, yet very God;
   From sin and death He saves us,
   And lightens ev'ry load.

LIPPAI

Traditional Tyrolean [GKE]

19th Century Tyrolean Carol [WE]

Allegretto moderato

1. Lip - pai, — steh — auf vom Schlaf! "Was____ ist denn da?" Mich
1. Lip - pai, — get — out of bed! "No,____ I'm a - sleep." There

1. Lip - pai, — steh — auf vom Schlaf!
1. Lip - pai, — get — out of bed!

wun - dert's — dass d' schla - fen kannst. "Ich____ schlaf____ schon."
nev - er was such a sleep - y - head! "Sleep - ing — deep."

Wun - dert's — dass d' Schla - fen kannst.
Nev - er — such a sleep - y - head!

Geh mit mir auf die Weid, Schau, was für wun-der geit.
There is a glow in the night From a great star shin-ing bright!

Lip-pai, komm, Lip-pai, komm,
Lip-pai, come, Lip-pai, come,

'S ist so licht wie am Tag. "Was wär das?"
See, it is bright as day! "What did you say?"

'S ist so licht wie am Tag.
See, it is bright as day!

2. Bethlehem heisst der Ort!
"Wer hat's gesagt?"
Ich hab's vom Engel g'hört
"Hast ihn gefragt?"
Ein Jungfrau keusch und rein
Soll seine Mutter sein,
Dort wo der Stern brinnt.
"Geh nur geschwind!"

2. He's born in Bethlehem.
"How do you know?"
The angels, I learned the place from them.
"They told you so?"
Mary, the blest mother mild,
Tenderly cares for her Child
There, 'neath the beaming star.
"Can it be far?"

3. So schön ist keins geborn
Wie das Kind!
Dass's auf dem Heu muss lieg'n
Is rechte Sünd!
Ich tu die Mutter frag'n
Ob ich's mit mir darf trag'n;
Ich hätt die grösste Freud.
"Du redst gescheit."

3. No sweeter, lovelier Babe
Could I name.
His bed nothing but a pile of hay,
O, what a shame!
Mary, if only I might
Hold the dear Savior tonight,
Pure joy I'd owe to you.
"Please let me, too!"

Die Hirten auf dem Felde

AS LATELY WE WATCHED

Traditional Austrian
Translation: Anonymous

19th Century Austrian Carol [WE]

Allegro

1. Auf, auf nun, ehs Hirten,— nid — schläft's ma so läng! De —
1. As late - ly we watched O'er — our — fields through the night, A —

nächt is ver - gän - ga, — Nun — dägt es jä schon.
star there was seen Of — such — glo - ri - ous light!

Schauts nuar — dä - hear! — Schauts nuar — dä - hear! Wia
All through — the — night, — An - gels — did — sing, In

fai - råzt dås Schtearn - dl _ Je _ len - ga je _ meahr.
car - ols so sweet Of _ the _ birth of a _ King.

2. *Zu Bethlehem druntn*
   Geht nida da Schain,
   Es muass jå was Englisch's
   Vaborg'n drunt sain;
   An ålda Schtoll,
   An ålda Schtoll,
   Dear schaint und glanzt
   Eng åls wiara Krystall!

3. *Drum geh' nur, main Sepl,*
   Und b'sinn dih nit lang!
   Stich ah a fast's Kiz'l
   Und wåg dr au'n Gång:
   Geh' nit vüll um,
   Geh' nit vüll um.
   Und ruk flugs dain Hiaderl
   Und schtöll dih fain frumm!

2. A King of such beauty
   Was ne'er before seen;
   And Mary, His mother,
   So like to a queen.
   Blest be the hour,
   Welcome the morn,
   For Christ, our dear Savior
   On earth now is born.

3. Then shepherds, be joyful,
   Salute your liege King;
   Let hills and dales ring
   To the song that ye sing:
   Blest be the hour,
   Welcome the morn,
   For Christ, our dear Savior,
   On earth now is born.

Es Wird Scho Glei Dumpa
THE TWILIGHT IS FALLING

Traditional Austrian [GKE]

Traditional Austrian [WE]

Andante

1. Es wird scho glei dumpa, es wird jå schon Nåcht. Drum

1. The twi - light is fall - ing, and on steals the night; I

kimm i zu Dir her, mein Hei - land auf d'Wåcht. Will

come to Thee, Je - sus, my Heav - en - ly Light. I

172

2. *Schliass zua deine Augerl in Ruah und in Fried,*
   Und gib ma zum Abschied dein Segn nur grad mit.
   Aft wird ja mei Schlaferl a sorgenlos sein.
   Aft kann i mi ruahli aufs Niederlegn freun.
   Hei, hei, hei, hei, schlaf süass, herzliabs-Kind!

2. Oh, close Thy tired eyes, now, and drift into sleep.
   Although I must leave Thee, Thy blessing I'll keep.
   I go to my slumber and rest without care,
   Because Thou art near me, my Savior so fair.
   Lullaby, lullaby—sweetly sleep, dearest Child.

DA DROBEN VOM BERGE
ABOVE, ON THE MOUNTAIN

Traditional Austrian [GKE]

Traditional Austrian [WE]

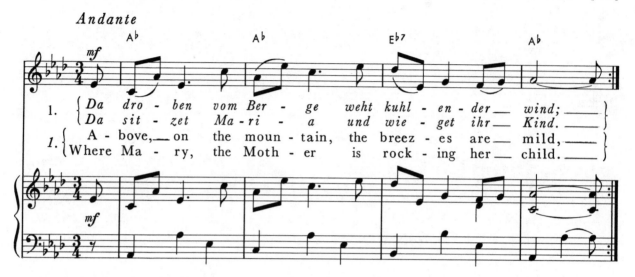

Andante

1. {
Da dro - ben vom Ber - ge weht kuhl - en - der wind;
Da sit - zet Ma - ri - a und wie - get ihr Kind.
}

1. {
A - bove, on the moun - tain, the breez - es are mild,
Where Ma - ry, the Moth - er is rock - ing her child.
}

Sie wiegt es mit ih - rer schnee - wei - ßen Hand, Drum

She rocks Him so gent - ly, and sweet - ly doth sing: "O

174

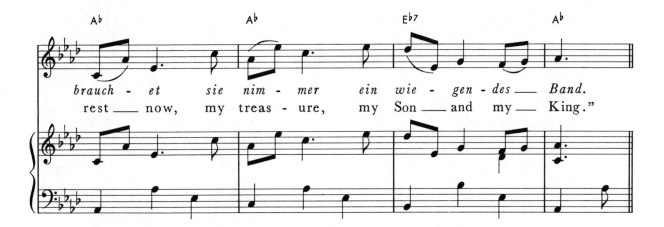

brauch - et sie nim - mer ein wie - gen - des___ Band.
rest___ now, my treas - ure, my Son___ and my___ King."

REFRAIN

Di-ri-di - ri, hal - le - lu - ja, hal-le - lu - ja, hal-le - lu - ja;Di-ri-di -
Di-ri-di - ri, hal - le - lu - ja, hal-le - lu - ja, hal-le - lu - ja;Di-ri-di -

ri, hal - le - lu - ja, hal-le - lu - ja, di-ri-di - ri. ___
ri; hal - le - lu - ja, hal-le - lu - ja, di-ri-di - ri. ___

2. *Das Kindlein erwachet, gen Himmel sie's
   hält,*
   Da singen die Englein, da singet die Welt:
   *Der Tod ist bezwungen, all Leid und
   Weh!*
   Geliebet, gelobet sei Gott in der Höh!
       Refrain

2. The Baby awakens and looks to the sky
   Where angels are singing their song from
     on high:
   "All praise to the almighty Father in
   Heav'n,
   And to all the earth may His great peace
     be giv'n."
       Refrain

175

Stille Nacht, Heilige Nacht

SILENT NIGHT, HOLY NIGHT

Joseph Mohr, 1818
Translation: Anonymous, from C.L. Hutchins'
    Sunday School Hymnal, 1871

Franz Gruber, 1818 [WE]

Larghetto

1. Stil - le nacht, Hei - li - ge nacht! Al - les schläft,
1. Si - lent night, Ho - ly night! All is calm,

1. Stil - le nacht, Hei - li - ge nacht, All' schläft,
1. Si - lent night, Ho - ly night all calm,

ein - sam wacht
All is bright

ein - sam wacht Nur das trau - te hoch - hei - li - ge Paar.
All is bright Round yon vir - gin Moth - er and Child.

2. *Stille Nacht, heilige Nacht!*
   Hirten erst kundgemacht!
   Durch der Engel Halleluja
   Tönt es laut von fern und nah:
   Christ, der Retter, ist da,
   Christ, der Retter, ist da!

3. *Stille Nacht, heilige Nacht!*
   Gottes Sohn, O, wie lacht
   Lieb aus deinem göttlichen Mund,
   Da uns schlägt die rettende Stund,
   Christ, in deiner Geburt,
   Christ, in deiner Geburt.

2. Silent night, holy night,
   Shepherds quake at the sight;
   Glories stream from heaven afar,
   Heavenly hosts sing alleluia,
   Christ, the Savior, is born!
   Christ, the Savior, is born!

3. Silent night, holy night,
   Son of God, love's pure light
   Radiant beams from Thy holy face,
   With the dawn of redeeming grace,
   Jesus, Lord, at Thy birth,
   Jesus, Lord, at Thy birth.

EIN KINDLEIN IN DER WIEGEN
A BABY IN THE CRADLE

D. G. Corner [GKE]

D. G. Corner
In Geistliche Nachtigal, Vienna, 1649 [WE]

1. Ein Kind - lein in der Wie - gen, Ein
1. A Ba - by in the cra - dle, A

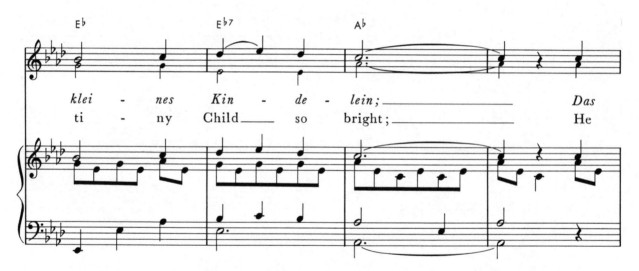

klei - nes Kin - de - lein; _____ Das
ti - ny Child___ so bright; _____ He

gleiß - et wie ein Spie - gel Nach
shin - eth as a mir - ror Re -

a — de - li — chem — Schein, _____ Das
flects a no - ble — light, _____ This

klei — ne Kin — de - lein. _____
ti — ny Child _____ so bright. _____

2. *Das Kindlein, das wir meinen*
   Das heisst: Herr Jesu Christ,
   Das verleih' uns Fried' und Einigkeit
   Wohl hie zu dieser Frist,
   Das geb' uns Jesu Christ!

3. *Und wer das Kindlein will wiegen,*
   Das kleine Kindelein,
   Der muss das nicht betrüben,
   Er muss demüthig sein
   Mit Maria der Jungfrau rein!

4. *O Jesu, liebstes Kindelein,*
   Du kleines Kindelein,
   Wie gross ist es die Liebe dein!
   Schleuss' in das Herze mein
   Die grosse Liebe dein!

2. The Child of whom we're speaking
   Is Jesus Christ, the Lord;
   He brings us peace and brotherhood
   If we but heed his word,
   Doth Jesus Christ, the Lord.

3. And he who rocks the cradle
   Of this sweet Child so fine
   Must serve with joy and heartiness,
   Be humble and be kind,
   For Mary's Child so fine.

4. O Jesus, dearest Savior,
   Although Thou art so small,
   With Thy great love o'erflowing
   Come flooding through·my soul,
   Thou lovely Babe so small.

STILL, STILL, STILL

Traditional Austrian [GKE]

Salzburg Melody, 1819 [WE]

Andante molto sostenuto

1. Still,___ still,___ still, Weil's _ Kind - lein schla - fen ___ will! Ma-
1. Still,___ still,___ still, He _ sleeps this _ night so ___ chill! The

ri - a _ tut es nie - der _ sin - gen, Ih - re __ keu - sche Brust dar - brin - gen,
Vir - gin's _ ten - der arms en - fold - ing, Warm and _ safe the Child are _ hold - ing,

Still,___ still,___ still, Weil __ Kind - lein __ schla - fen ___ will.
Still,___ still,___ still, He __ sleeps this __ night so ___ chill.

2. *Schlaf, schlaf, schlaf,*
   Mein liebes Kindlein, schlaf!
   Die Engel tuan schö musizieren,
   Bei dem Kindlein jubilieren,
   Schlaf, schlaf, schlaf,
   Mein liebes Kindlein, schlaf!

2. Sleep, sleep, sleep,
   He lies in slumber deep
   While angel hosts from heav'n come
     winging,
   Sweetest songs of joy are singing,
   Sleep, sleep, sleep,
   He lies in slumber deep.

Gloria

Traditional Austrian [GKE]

Austrian Carol [WE]

Allegretto

1. *Glo - ri - a, Glo - ri - a, Gott in der Höh,*
1. "Glo - ri - a, Glo - ri - a, To God on high!"

Sing - en die En - ge - lein, Sing - en so lieb und fein:
How sweet - ly an - gel songs Ring through the win - ter sky:

Glo - ri - a, Glo - ri - a, Gott in der Höh.
"Glo - ri - a, Glo - ri - a, To God on high!"

De Nederige Geboorte
THE SIMPLE BIRTH

Traditional Flemish [GKE]

Traditional Flemish [WE]

1. Er   is   een   kin-de-kin   ge-bo-ren   op   d'aard':   Er

1. From Heav'n   there   came to earth   a   Ba-by   so   small: From

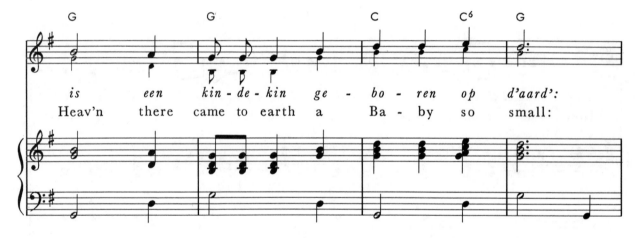

is   een   kin-de-kin   ge-bo-ren   op   d'aard':

Heav'n   there   came to earth   a   Ba-by   so   small:

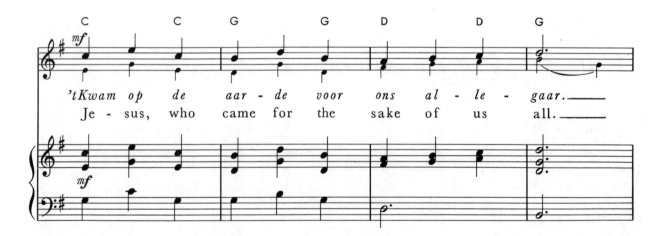

'tKwam   op   de   aar-de   voor   ons   al-le-gaar.____

Je-sus,   who   came   for   the   sake   of   us   all.____

'*t Kwam op de aar - de voor ons al - le - gaar.*
Je - sus, who came for the sake of us all.

2. *Er is een kindekin geboren in 't strooi,*
   't Lag in een kribbetje gedekt met hooi.

3. *'t Had twee schoon oogjes, zoo zwart als laget,*
   Twee bleusende kaakjes, dat stond hem zoo net.

4. *'t Keek naar zijn moeder en 't lachte zoo snel,*
   't Kende de liefde zijns moeders zoo wel.

5. *'t Kwam op de aarde voor ons allegaar,*
   En 't wenscht ons een zalig nieuwe jaar.

2. Beneath His tiny head no pillow but hay;
   God's richest treasure in rude manger lay.

3. His eyes of blackest jet were sparkling with light,
   Rosy cheeks bloomed on His face fair and bright.

4. And from His lovely mouth, the laughter did swell,
   When He saw Mary, whom He loved so well.

5. He came to weary earth, so dark and so drear,
   To wish to mankind a blessed New Year.

Ons Is Geboren Een Kindekin
TODAY WE WELCOME A TINY CHILD

Traditional 14th Century Dutch [GKE]

Traditional 14th Century Dutch [WE]

Andante

1. Ons is ge - bo - ren een kin - de - kin, Noch
1. To - day we wel - come a ti - ny Child That

clae - re dan die son - ne; Dat sal hun al - len
pales the sun's bright shin - ing; Our hope and joy, this

vrou - de sijn Al tot der on - ge - len won - ne.
In - fant mild, Whom an - gel songs are en - shrin - ing.

2. *Die sterren gheven ons lichten schijn*
   All door den hemel gedroughen;
   Maria die heeft haer lieve kint
   Mit ganser minnen ghewonnen.

2. The stars that spangle the radiant sky
   Announce the gift from Heaven,
   While Mary adores her Holy Boy
   That God the Father has given.

184

SCANDINAVIAN CAROLS

Det Kimer Nu Til Julefest

THE HAPPY CHRISTMAS COMES ONCE MORE

Nicolai F.S. Grundtvig, 1817
Translation: C.P. Krauth, 1867

C. Balle, 1850 [WE]

Allegretto

1. Det___ ki - mer nu til ju - le - fest, Det
1. The___ hap - py Christ - mas comes___ once more, The

ki - mer for den___ høi - e gjest, Som
heav'n - ly Guest is___ at___ the door, The

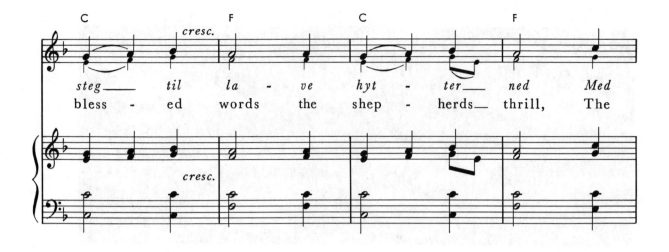

steg___ til la - ve hyt - ter___ ned Med
bless - ed words the shep - herds___ thrill, The

nytt - aars - ga - ver: fryd___ og___ fred.
joy - ous ti - dings, peace,___ good___ will.

2. *O kom da med til Davids by,*
   Hvor engler synger under sky!
   O følg med oss paa marken ud,
   Hvor hyrder hører nytt fra Gud!

3. *Og la oss gaa med stille sinn,*
   Som hyrdene til barnet inn,
   Med gledestaarer takke Gud
   For miskunnhet og naadebud.

4. *Kom, Jesus, vaer vor hyttes gjest,*
   Hold selv i oss din julefest
   Da skal med Davidsharpens klang
   Dig takke høit vor julesang.

2. To David's city let us fly,
   Where angels sing beneath the sky,
   Through plain and village pressing near,
   And news from God with shepherds hear.

3. O, let us go with quiet mind,
   The gentle Babe with shepherds find,
   To gaze on Him who gladdens them,
   The loveliest flow'r on Jesse's stem.

4. Come, Jesus, glorious heav'nly guest,
   Keep Thine own Christmas in our breast;
   Then David's harp-string, hushed so long
   Shall swell our jubilee of song.

Deilig Er den Himmel Blaa
LOVELY IS THE DARK BLUE SKY

Nicolai F.S. Grundtvig, 1783–1872 [GKE]

Traditional Danish [WE]

Allegro moderato

1. Dei - lig er den him-mel blaa, Lyst det er at se der-paa,
1. Love - ly is the dark blue sky, Beau - ti - ful to ev - 'ry eye,

Hvor de gyld-ne stjer - ner blin - ker, Hvor de smi - ler, hvor de vin - ker
Where the gold - en stars are blink-ing, See them smil-ing, see them wink-ing

Os fra jor-den op til sig, Os fra jor-den op til sig.
Beck-'ning us to Heav'n on high, Beck-'ning us to Heav'n on high.

2. *Det var midt i julenat,*
   Hver en stierne glimtet matt;
   Men med ett der blev at skue
   En saa klar paa himlens bue,
   Som en liten stjernesol,
   Som en liten stjernesol.

3. *Østerlands de vise menn*
   Fandt dog stjernen der igjen,
   Some de skuet i det høie;
   Ti i barnets milde øie
   Funklende og klar den sat,
   Funklende og klar den sat.

2. On the earliest Christmas night,
   All the stars were shining bright,
   When, among them, burst in brilliance
   One lone star whose streaming radiance
   Far surpassed the sun's own light,
   Far surpassed the sun's own light.

3. Wise men from the East afar,
   Led to Jesus by the star,
   There adoring Heav'n's elected,
   Found within his eyes reflected
   God's great Light, and Love, and Pow'r.
   God's great Light, and Love, and Pow'r.

Barn Jesus

CHILD JESUS

Hans Christian Andersen, 1805–1875 [GKE]

Niels Gade, 1817–1890 [WE]

1. Barn Je-sus i en Kryb-be laa, Skjønt Him-len var hans
1. Child Je-sus in a man-ger lay, Yet Heav-en was His

Ej - e, Hans Pu-de her blev Hø of Straa, Morkt
own. His low-ly pil-low was of straw, And

var det om hans Lej - e; Men Stjer-nen o - ver
round Him no light shone; But in the sky the

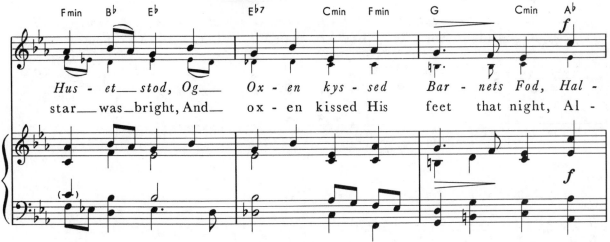

Hus - et stod, Og Ox - en kys - sed Bar - nets Fod, Hal -
star was bright, And ox - en kissed His feet that night, Al -

le - lu - jah, Hal - le - lu - jah, Hal - le - lu - jah!
le - lu - jah, Al - le - lu - jah, Al - le - lu - jah!

2. *Hver sorgfuld Sjael, bliv karsk og glad,*
   Ryst af din tunge Smerte,
   Et Barn er født i Davids Stad,
   Til Trøst for hvert et Hjerte;
   Til Barnet vil vi stige ind
   Og blive, Børn i Sjael og Sind.
   Halleluja, Halleluja, Halleluja!

3. O sorrowing soul, be glad today,
   Cast out your bitter pain;
   For Bethle'm's Babe will show the way
   We heav'nly bliss can gain.
   Let us with childlike heart and mind
   Seek now the Son of God to find.
   Alleluia, Alleluia, Alleluia!

ET BARN ER FØDT I BETLEHEM
A CHILD IS BORN IN BETHLEHEM

Nicolai F.S. Grundtvig, 1783–1872 [GKE]
Based on 14th Century Latin Text

Traditional Danish Carol [WE]

1. Et barn er født i Bet-le-hem, i Bet-le-hem, Ti
1. A child is born in Beth-le-hem, in Beth-le-hem; And

gle-der sig Je-ru-sa-lem. Al-le-lu-ja, al-le-lu-ja!
joy is in Je-ru-sa-lem, Al-le-lu-ja, al-le-lu-ja!

2. *En fattig jomfru sat i løn,*
   Hun sat i løn,
   Og fødte himlens kongesøn.
   Alleluia, alleluia!

2. A lowly maiden all alone,
   So all alone,
   Gave birth to God's own Holy Son.
   Alleluia, alleluia!

3. *Han lagdes i et krybberum,*
   Et krybberum;
   Guds engler sang med fryd derom.
   Alleluia, alleluia!

3. She chose a manger for His bed,
   For Jesus' bed.
   God's angels sang for joy o'erhead,
   Alleluia, alleluia!

4. *Lov, tak og pris i evighet,*
   I evighet,
   Den hellige trefoldighet.
   Alleluia, alleluia!

4. Give thanks and praise eternally,
   Eternally,
   To God, the Holy Trinity.
   Alleluia, alleluia!

Nu Är Det Jul Igen
YULETIDE IS HERE AGAIN

Traditional Swedish [GKE]

Swedish Dance Carol [WE]

Allegro moderato

1. Nu är det Jul i - gen, och nu är det Jul i - gen, Och
1. Yule-tide is here a - gain, the yule-tide is here a - gain, We'll

Ju - len va - ra ska' till Pas - ka. Sa är det Pask i - gen, och
dance and cel - e - brate till Eas - ter. Then, when it's Eas-ter-time, Yes

sa är det Pask i - gen, Och Pask - en va - ra ska' till Ju - la.
then when it's Eas - ter-time, We'll dance and cel - e - brate till Christ-mas.

2. Nu är det Jul igen, och nu är det Jul
   igen,
  Och Julen vara ska' till Paska.
  Det var inte sant, och det var inte sant,
  For där emellan kommer Fastan.

2. Yuletide is here again, the yuletide is here
   again,
  We'll dance and celebrate till Easter.
  Ev'ryone knows this cannot really be so
  Because of Lent, when we must all be
   fasting.

Nar Juldagsmorgon Glimmar

WHEN CHRISTMAS MORN IS DAWNING

Traditional Swedish [GKE]

German Folk Song, 1823 [WE]

Andante moderato

1. När jul-dags-mor-gon glim-mar, Jag vill till stal-let ga, Der
1. When Christ-mas morn is dawn-ing, In hum-ble faith I'd go To

Gud i nat-tens tim-mar Re'n hvi-lar up-pa stra. Der
Beth-le-hem, and see___ Him That lies up-on the straw. To

Gud i nat-tens tim-mar Re'n hvi-lar up-pa stra.
Beth-le-hem, and see___ Him That lies up on the straw.

194

2. *Hur god du var, som ville*
   Till jorden komma ner!
   Nu ej i synd jag spille
   Min bardoms dagar mer!

3. *Dig, Jesus, vi behöfva,*
   Du käre barnavän!
   Jag vill ej mer befröfva
   Med synder dig igen!

2. How good of You, my Savior,
   To come from Heav'n above!
   O take away my sinning,
   Protect me with Thy love.

3. Blest Jesus, how I need Thee,
   The children's dearest friend!
   O may I never grieve Thee
   With pain of sin again.

Her Kommer Dine Arme Smaa

THY LITTLE ONES, DEAR LORD, ARE WE

Hans Adolf Brorson, 1732
Translation: Harriet R. Spaeth, 1898

J.A.P. Schulz, 1747–1800 [WE]

1. Her___ kom-mer di - ne ar - me smaa, O___ Je - sus, i din

1. Thy___ lit - tle ones, dear Lord, are we, And___ come Thy low - ly

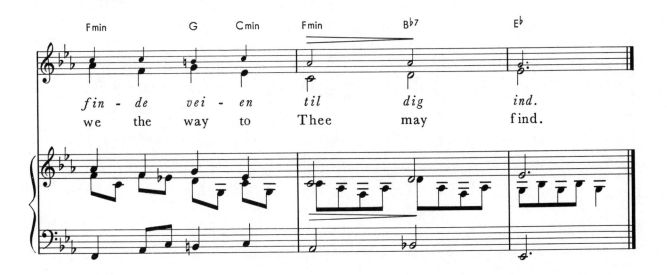

2. *Vi løper dig med sang imot,*
   Og kysser støvet for din fot;
   O salig stund, O søte nat,
   Da du blev født, vor sjeleskat!

3. *Saa drag og ganske til dig hen,*
   Du store, milde sjeleven,
   Saa vi i troon favner dig
   Og følger paa din himmelveg!

4. *Her staar vi nu i flok og rad,*
   Om dig, vort skjønne hjerteblad,
   Ak hjelp at vi og alle maa
   I himlen for din trone staa!

2. With songs we hasten Thee to great,
   And kiss the dust before Thy feet,
   O blessed hour, O sweetest night,
   That gave Thee birth, our soul's delight!

3. O draw us wholly to Thee, Lord,
   Do Thou to us Thy grace accord,
   True faith and love to us impart,
   That we may hold Thee in our heart.

4. We gather round Thee, Jesus dear,
   So happy in Thy presence here;
   Grant us, our Savior, ev'ry one,
   To stand in Heav'n before Thy throne.

Du Grønne, Glitrende Tre, God-Dag

YOU GREEN AND GLITTERING TREE, GOOD DAY

Johan Krohn [GKE]

C.E.F. Weyse [WE]

1. Du grøn-ne, glit-ren-de tre,— god-dag! Vel-kom-men, du som vi ser saa gjer-ne, Med jul-le-lys og med nor-ske flag Og høit i top-pen den blan-ke stjer-ne! Ja, den maa skin-ne, for

1. You green and glit-ter-ing tree,— good day! With joy— and glad-ness we hail your com-ing; Be-decked with can-dles and span-gles gay, Your top-most star is as sun-light dawn-ing! Our hearts' re-mind-er, of

den skal min-ne, Ja den maa skin-ne, for den skal min-ne, Os
Heav-en's splen-dor, Our hearts' re-mind-er of Heav-en's splen-dor, And

om___ vor___ Gud,___ Os om vor God.___
God's___ great___ love,___ And God's great love.___

2. *Den første jul i et fremmed land*
   Sin store stjerne Vorherre tendte;
   Den skulde vise vor jord at han
   Den lille Jesus till verden sendte:
   I stjerneglansen gik engledansen,
   I stjerneglansen gik engledansen,
   Om Betlehem, om Betlehem.

2. When Jesus came to the earth that day,
   The largest star in the sky He lighted;
   He gave a beacon to show the way
   To ev'ry soul, His salvation plighted.
   Above Him singing, the angels winging,
   Above Him singing, the angels winging,
   O'er Bethlehem, o'er Bethlehem.

3. *Om Jesusbarnet fortalte mor*
   Saa mangen aften vi sat her hjemme;
   Kan hans bud og hans milde ord,
   Vi vet at aldrig vi dem maa glemme.
   Naar stjernen skinner, om ham os minner,
   Naar stjernen skinner, om ham os minner
   Vort juletre, vort juletre.

3. Oft-times at evening in our old home,
   Our dearest Mother would tell the story
   Of Jesus' love, and his words sublime—
   The mem'ry fills our hearts with glory.
   The tree in splendor our heart's reminder,
   The tree in splendor our heart's reminder
   Of God's great love, of God's great love.

O Jul Med Din Glede

O CHRISTMAS, YOU SEASON OF CHILDLIKE DELIGHT

Gustava Kielland [GKE]

Traditional Norwegian [WE]

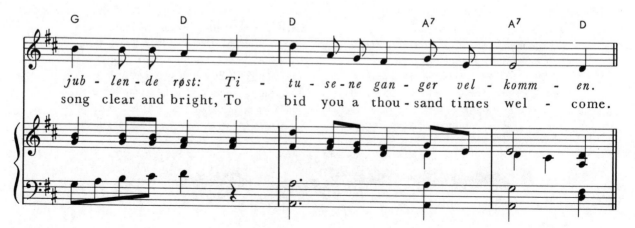

Vi klap-per i hen - de - ne, Vi syn-ger og vi ler, Saa glad-e - lig, saa
Our hands we will clap, clap, clap, As mer-ry as can be; So glad are we this

glad - e - lig, Vi swing-er oss i kret - sen, og nei - er.
day to see We swing a-round a cir - cle, and curt - sey.

2. I Østerlands vise, I tre stjernemenn,
   Vi vet jo nok hvorhen I drage;
   Ti vi vilde ogsaa gjerne derhen
   Og eder paa reisen ledsage.
       Refrain

2. O wise men who come from the lands of
   of the East,
   We know of the Babe you are seeking;
   We pray we may join you in your holy
       quest,
   And follow the star brightly beaming.
       Refrain

3. Saa rekker jeg dig nu med glede min
       haand,
   Kom skynd dig og gi mig den anden.
   Saa knytter vi kjaerlighets hellige baand
   Og lover at elske hinanden.
       Refrain

3. In joy and thanksgiving I offer my hand,
   And ask that you give yours in token,
   That we be united by this sacred band:
   God's love through the ages unbroken.
       Refrain

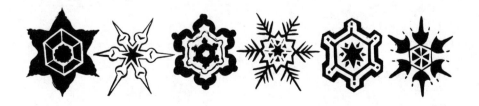

201

Jeg Er Saa Glad Hver Julekveld
I AM SO GLAD ON CHRISTMAS EVE

Marie Wexelsen, 1832–1911 [GKE]

Peder Knudsen, 1819–1863 [WE]

1. Jeg er saa glad hver julekveld Ti da blev Jesus født, ___ Da lyste stjernen som en sol, Og engle sang ___ saa sødt. ___

1. I am so glad on Christmas Eve, The night of Jesus' birth; ___ The night the Star ___ shone like the sun, And angels sang ___ on earth. ___

2. Jeg er saa glad hver julekveld
   Da synger vi hans pris,
   Da aapner han for alle smaa
   Sit søde paradis.

2. I am so glad on Christmas Eve.
   Our grateful praises rise
   To Jesus, who has opened wide
   His own sweet Paradise.

SLAVIC CAROLS

W Zlobie Lezy

JESUS HOLY, BORN SO LOWLY

Traditional Polish [GKE]

Traditional Polish [WE]

1. W zlo-bie le - zy ktoz po-bie - zy lo-len-do-wac Ma-le-mu.
1. Je-sus ho - ly, born so low - ly, We will sing you car-ols gay.

Je-zu-so - wi, Chrys-tu-so - wi, Dzis nam na - ro - dzo-ne-mu.
Je-sus dear - est, pre-cious In - fant, Come to us from Heav'n to -day.

Pa - stu-szko-wie przy-by waj - cie, Je - mu piek-nie

Shep - herds, join the joy-ful cho - rus, Heav'n - ly love is

przy-gry-waj - cie, Ja - ko Pa - nu na-sze-mu.

reign-ing o'er___ us, Here ap-pear - ing as a Babe.

Ja - ko Pa - nu na-sze - mu.

Here ap-pear-ing as a Babe.

2. *My zas sami, z piosneczkami,*
Za wami pospieszymy.
A tak tego Malenkiego
Niech wszyscy zobaczymy.
Jak ubogo narodzony,
Placze w stajni polozony
Wiec go dzis ucieszymy.

2. On the straw the Babe is sleeping,
In the humble manger bed.
Mary loving watch is keeping,
Angels hover 'round His head.
Shepherds bow in adoration,
Praising God's sweet benediction
That upon the earth is shed.

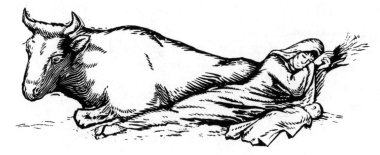

Dziasiaj w Betlejem

O COME REJOICING

Traditional Polish [GKE]

Traditional Polish [WE]

Allegretto

1. Dzi-siaj wBe-tle-hem, dzi-siaj wBe-tle-jem Wie-so-la no-wi-na,
1. O, come re-joic-ing, O, come re-joic-ing Beth-le-hem, re-joice ye!

Ze Pan-na czys-ta ze Pan-na czys-ta po-ro-dzi-la sy-na.
For of a Vir-gin, for of a Vir-gin God is born un-to thee!

REFRAIN

Chrys - tus sie ro - dzi, Pan os - wo - bo - dzi A - nie - li gra - ja,
Tru - ly He com-eth, Christ, our sal - va - tion, An - gels are voic - ing

Kro - le wi - ta - ja, Pa - ster - ze spie - wa - ja, By - dle - ta kle - ka - ja
Their ju - bi - la - tion; Shep-herds come to praise Him, Ox - en kneel be - fore Him,

Cu - da, cu - da og - la - sza - ja.
What a Won - der God ——— has giv'n!

2. *Maryja Panna, Maryja Panna,*
   Dzieciatko piastuje
   A Jozef Stary, A Jozef Stary,
   Ono pielegnuje
       Refrain

2. Mary is singing, Mary is singing
   Songs for Thee, dear Jesus;
   Joseph is watching, Joseph is watching
   O'er the Son so glorious.
       Refrain

207

O Gwiazdo Betlejemska
O STAR O'ER BETHLEHEM SHINING

Traditional Polish [GKE]

Traditional Polish [WE]

Andante

mp

1. O gwiaz - do Be - tle - jem - ska zas-wiec na mem nie - bie Ja
1. O star o'er Beth-le-hem shin - ing, Bring me your heav'n-ly light; For

cie szu-kam wsrod no - cy Ja te-sknie do Cie - bie. Pro-
long my heart has been pin - ing, Seek-ing you through the night. Come,

208

wadz mnie do ___ sta - jen - ki   Gdzie Chry - stus zlo - zo-
lead me to ___ the sta - ble,   There, to the man - ger

ny ___ Bog czlo - wiek z Pan - ny swie - tej ___
bed ___ Where Je - sus, in gar - ments low - ly, ___

Dla nas na - ro - dzo - ny. ___   Pro - ny. ___
Pil - lows His ti - ny head. ___   Come, head. ___

Gdy Sie Chrystus Rodzi

CHRIST IS BORN THIS EVENING

Traditional Polish [GKE]   Traditional Polish [WE]

1. Gdy sie Chrys-tus ro-dzi, I na swiat przy-cho-dzi.
1. Christ is born this eve-ning, Let us go re-joic-ing!

Ciem-na noc w jas-no-sciach Pro-mie-nis-tych bro-dzi.
Though the night is gloom-y, Day will soon be dawn-ing!

A-nio-lo-wie sie ra-du-ja, pod nie-bio-sa wy spie-wu-ja:
An-gels from on high are sing-ing To the One who comes from Heav-en:

210

"Glo - ri - a, Glo - ri - a, Glo - ri - a,
"Glo - ri - a, Glo - ri - a, Glo - ri - a,

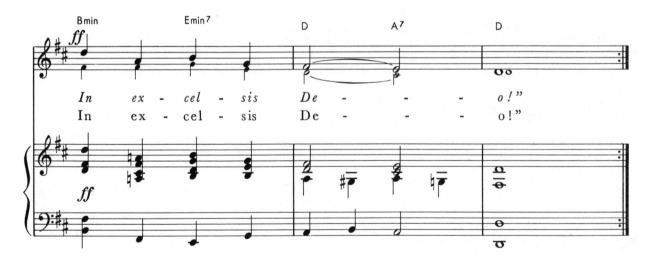

In ex - cel - sis De - - - o!"
In ex - cel - sis De - - - o!"

2. *Mowia do pasterzy*
   Ktorzy trzod swych strzeggli,
   Aby do Betlejem
   Czempredzej pobiegli
   Bo sie narodzil Zbawiciel,
   Wszego swiata adkupiciel.
   Gloria, gloria, gloria,
   In excelsis Deo!

2. Shepherds, hasten yonder,
   Where the Babe most holy,
   In this cold December,
   Lies in manger lowly.
   See, the star on high is gleaming,
   O'er the lovely Infant beaming!
   Gloria, gloria, gloria,
   In excelsis Deo!

Przybiezeli do Betlejem
SHEPHERDS CAME TO BETHLEHEM

Traditional Polish [GKE]

Traditional Polish [WE]

Allegro vivace

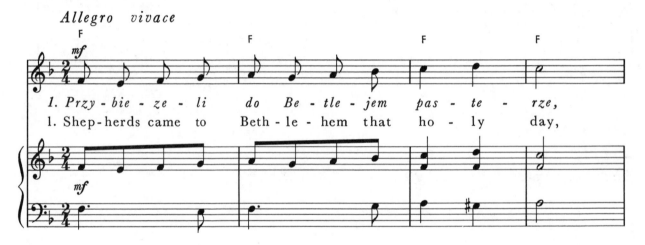

1. *Przy - bie - ze - li   do Be - tle - jem   pas - te - rze,*
1. Shep-herds came to   Beth - le - hem that   ho - ly   day,

Gra - ja   sko - cznie   dzie - cia - tecz - ku   na   li - rze.
For the   ba - by   Je - sus on   the   lyres   did   play.

1. Wi - ta - ja dzie-cia-tko, ma - le ___ pa-cho-lat-ko,
1. How great their thank-ful-ness and joy To ___ see the Vir-gin's

Pa - ste - rze, pa - ste - rze.
love - ly Boy! Heav'n - ly joy!

2. *Dzieciatko sie do pastuszkow usmiecha*
   Jako Jesus czystem sercem oddycha,
   Chwala na wysokosci,
   Chwala na wysokosci,
   A pokoj na ziemi.

2. And the Baby Jesus smiled upon them all,
   Happy with the notes that on His ears did
   fall.
   Glory to God in highest Heaven,
   Peace on earth, good will to men!
   Peace from Heaven.

MIZERNA CICHA

ONLY A MANGER BED

Traditional Polish [GKE]   Traditional Polish [WE]

1. Mi - zer - na, ci - cha, sta - jen - ka li - cha, Pel - na nie - bies - kiej chwa - ly, __ O - to le - za - cy na sia - nie spia - cy, Wprom - ien - iach Je - zus ma - ly.

1. On - ly a man - ger bed for the Stran - ger Sent down from Heav - en to save __ us! __ But Love is keep - ing watch as He's sleep - ing, Dear Son of God, most glo - rious!

214

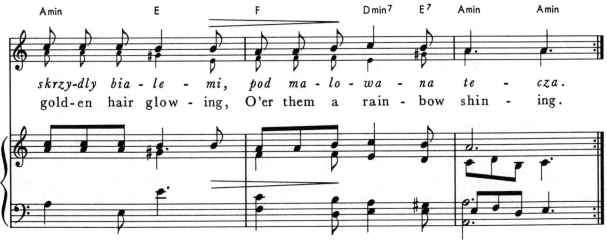

Sliczna Panienka

CAROL OF THE HAY

Traditional Polish [GKE]

Traditional Polish [WE]

216

REFRAIN

O sia - no, sia - no, Sia - no jak li - li - ja,
Fresh hay, O fresh hay, Fra-grant as the lil - y!

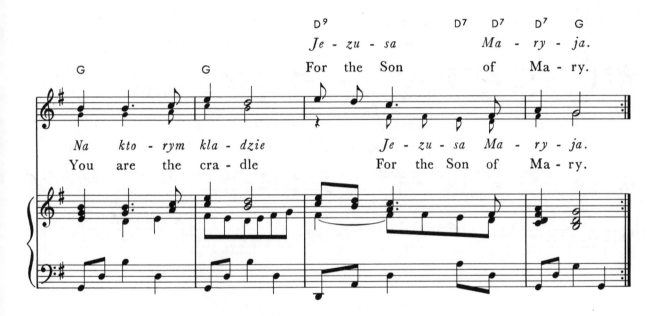

Je - zu - sa Ma - ry - ja.
For the Son of Ma - ry.

Na kto - rym kla - dzie Je - zu - sa Ma - ry - ja.
You are the cra - dle For the Son of Ma - ry.

217

Wsrod Nocnej Ciszy
IN MIDNIGHT'S SILENCE

Traditional Polish [GKE]

Traditional Polish [WE]

Moderato

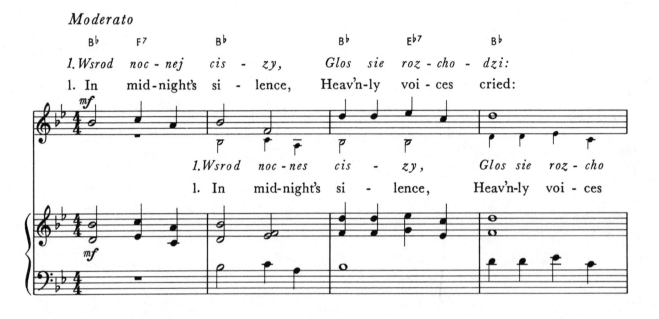

1. Wsrod noc-nej cis - zy, Glos sie roz-cho-dzi:
1. In mid-night's si - lence, Heav'n-ly voi - ces cried:

1. Wsrod noc-nes cis - zy, Glos sie roz-cho
1. In mid-night's si - lence, Heav'n-ly voi - ces

"Wstan - cie pas - te - rze, Bog sie wam ro - dzi.
"Rise up, O shep - herds, Christ is born to - night!

dzi: "Wstan - cie pas - te - rze, Bog sie wam ro
cried: "Rise up, O shep - herds, Christ is born to -

2. *Pozli, znalezli*
   Dzieciatko w zlobie,
   Wszyslkiemi znaki
   Danemi sobie.
   Jako Bogu czesc mu dali,
   A witajac zawolali
   Z wielkiej radosci,
   Z wielkiej radosci.

2. Shepherds came running
   From the fields afar,
   To Jesus' cradle,
   Following the star.
   Kneeling there in adoration,
   They cried out in exultation:
   "Praise to God on high,
   Praise to God on high."

Lulajze Jezuniu
POLISH LULLABY

Traditional Polish [GKE]　　　　　　　　　　　　　　Traditional Polish [WE]

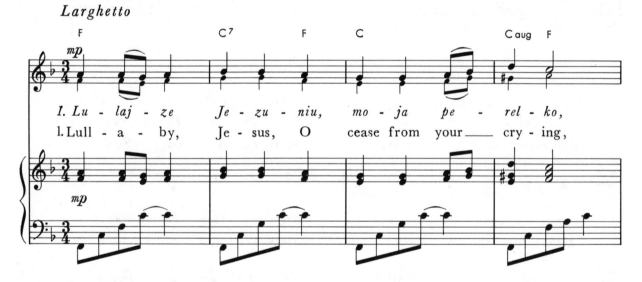

1. Lu - laj - ze　Je - zu - niu,　mo - ja　pe - rel - ko,

1. Lull - a - by,　Je - sus,　O　cease from your____ cry - ing,

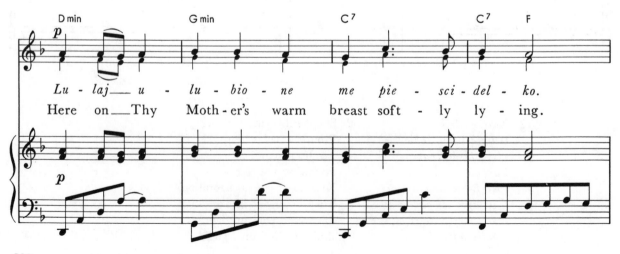

Lu - laj____ u - lu - bio - ne　me pie - sci - del - ko.

Here on____ Thy　Moth - er's　warm　breast soft - ly　ly - ing.

Lu - laj - ze — Je - zu - niu, — lu - laj - ze lu - laj,
Lull - a - by, — Je - sus, — O — sleep now, my treas - ure,

A Ty — Go Ma - tu - lu w pla - czu u - tu - laj.
Moth - er — is watch - ing with love none can meas - ure.

2. *Wejrz okiem laskawem, ma swiat ten caly,*
   Blogoslaw go raczka, Jezuniu maly.
   Lulajze Jezuniu, lulajze lulaj,
   A Ty Go Matulu wplaczu utulaj.

2. See how the world lies in sorrow and
   sadness;
   Give us Thy blessing, O bring Heaven's
   gladness!
   Lullaby, Jesus, O sleep now, my treasure;
   Mother is watching with love none can
   measure.

POCHVALEN BUD', JEZIS KRISTUS

PRAISE TO JESUS, OUR SALVATION

Traditional Czech [GKE]   Traditional Czech [WE]

Allegretto moderato

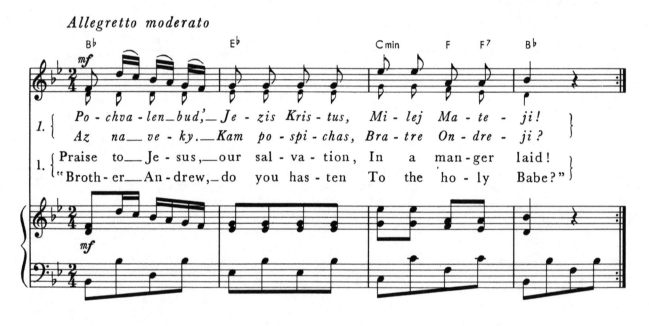

1. Po - chva - len bud', Je - zis Kris - tus, Mi - lej Ma - te - ji!
   Az na ve - ky. Kam po - spi - chas, Bra - tre On - dre - ji?

1. Praise to Je - sus, our sal - va - tion, In a man - ger laid!
   "Broth - er An - drew, do you has - ten To the ho - ly Babe?"

"Ja do Be - tle - ma be - zim, Co se tam sta - lo, ne - vim,
"Yea, to Beth - le - hem I go, Since the an - gel song I know;

222

Bro - sim, — bra - tre, — vrat' se   se   mnou,   Ne - co   ti   po - vim. ——— "
Through the — strange — and — mys - tic wea - ther,   Let   us   go   to - geth - er."

2. *Nasi hosi vecir pasli*
   Blizko Betlema,
   Velka jasnost na obloze
   Jako den byla.
   Andelsky zpez slyseli,
   Do Betlema bozoli,
   Zo so narodil Kristus Pan,
   Pravdu mluvili.

2. We were herding in the evening,
   Near to Bethlehem,
   When a great light o'er us streaming,
   Frightened ev'ry man.
   Angel hosts all robed in white
   Hymns were singing in the night,
   Of an Infant come from Heaven
   Down to earth this evening.

3. *Nechod'me tam jako blazni,*
   Milej Ondreji,
   Aby sme tam nesli prazdni,
   Kdyz nic nemaji.
   Pod'me pro kamarady,
   Naberem s sebou dary,
   Az toho trosku shledame,
   Pujdem spesmeji.

3. "Andrew, not so fast, I'm begging,
   Stop and take your ease!
   Simple gifts we should be bearing,
   That the Babe would please.
   Likely they are very poor;
   We could spare some from our store,
   For the Baby and his father,
   And the Virgin Mother."

4. *Vzhuru, bratri, kamaradi,*
   Budeme hrati!
   Kdepak jsou ty male deti,
   At' jdou zpivati.
   Franto, piskej klar'nety,
   Ondreji, vem valdhorny,
   Tadyasi, polni trouby,
   A Nacku, bubny!

4. What a crowd around us gathered,
   Looking at the Babe!
   Bring the little children hither,
   Have them sing His praise.
   On our instruments we'll play,
   Celebrating this great day,
   When the Son of God appearing
   Conquers all our fearing!

Pujdem Spolu Do Betlema

WE ARE GOING TO THE STABLE

Traditional Czech [GKE]   Traditional Czech [WE]

Allegretto

1. Puj-dem spo-lu do Bet-le-ma, Duj-daj,—duj-daj,— duj-daj,—da!

1. We are go-ing to the sta-ble Duj-daj,—duj-daj,— duj-daj,—da!

Je - žiš - ku, pa - nač - ku! Ja te bu - du ko - li - ba - ti,
Je - sus we there will see, And His cra - dle we'll be rock - ing,

Je - žiš - ku, pa - nač - ku! Ja te bu - du ko - li - bat.
Je - sus we there will see, And we all will shout with glee!

2. *Zachi, Kubo, na ty dudy:*
   Dujdaj, dujdaj, dujdaj da!
   Refrain

3. *A ty, Janku, na pist'alu:*
   Dudli, tudli, dudli da!
   Refrain

4. *A ty Miksi, na houslicky:*
   Hudli, tydli, hudli da!
   Refrain

5. *A ty, Vavro, na tu basu:*
   Rum-rum, rum-rum, rum-a da!
   Refrain

2. You start, Jacob, on the bagpipe,
   Dujdaj, dujdaj, dujdaj da!
   Refrain

3. John, you play upon your whistle,
   Dudli, tudli, dudli da!
   Refrain

4. Matthew, tune up on your fiddle,
   Hudli, tydli, hudli da!
   Refrain

5. Jamie, chime in with your tuba,
   Rum-rum, rum-rum, rum-a da!
   Refrain

Hajej, Nynej, Ježišku
ROCKING CAROL

Traditional Czech [GKE]   Traditional Czech [WE]

Music arrangement used by permission of C. A. Scholin Publishing Co., St Louis, Mo.

Bu - de - me — tě ko - li - ba - ti, A - bys moh' li - be po - spa - ti,
We will rock You, rock You, rock You, Gent - ly slum - ber — as we rock You,

Ha - jej, ny - nej Je - ži - ku, Pu - či - me ti — ko - ži - ku.
Je - sus, Je - sus, do not — fear, We who — love You — will — be — near.

2. Hajej, nynej, milačku, milačku,
   Mariansky synačku.
   Budeme tě kolibaři,
   Abys moh' libe pospati,
   Hajej, nynej, milačku,
   Mariansky synačku.

2. Jesus, Jesus, darling One, darling One,
   Gift of Heaven, Mary's Son,
   We will rock You, rock You, rock You,
   Gently slumber as we rock You;
   Jesus, Jesus, do not fear,
   We who love You will be near.

SLYŠELI JSME V BETLEMĚ
WE HAVE HEARD IN BETHLEHEM

Traditional Czech [GKE]

Traditional Czech [WE]

Andante

1. Sly - še - li jsme vBe - tle - mě,

1. We have ___ heard in ___ Beth - le - hem,

Že tam ___ le - ži ___ na ___ se - ně. To pře -

Lies a ___ Babe, a ___ heav'n - ly ___ gem. O'er the

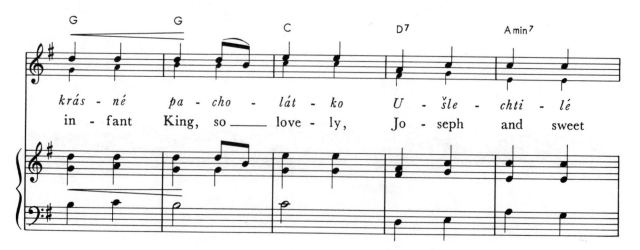

krás - né pa - cho - lát - ko U - šle - chti - lé

in - fant King, so ___ love - ly, Jo - seph and sweet

228

Je - zu - lát - ko, ___ Jo - sef ___ smat - kou ___ je ___ hlí -
Ma - ry ___ hov - 'ring, ___ We have ___ heard in ___ Beth - le -

dá, Jo - sef ___ smat - kou ___ je ___ hlí - dá.
hem, Lies a ___ Babe, a ___ heav'n - ly ___ gem.

229

Zezulka z Lesa Vylítla

FROM OUT THE FOREST A CUCKOO FLEW

Traditional Czech [GKE]

Traditional Czech [WE]

1. Ze - zul - ka z le - sa vy - lít - la, Ku - ku!
1. From out the for - est a cuck - oo flew, Cuck - oo!

U sa - mých je - sli - ček sed - la, Ku - ku! Vzdá -
Seek - ing the heav - en - ly Babe to woo, Cuck - oo! Near

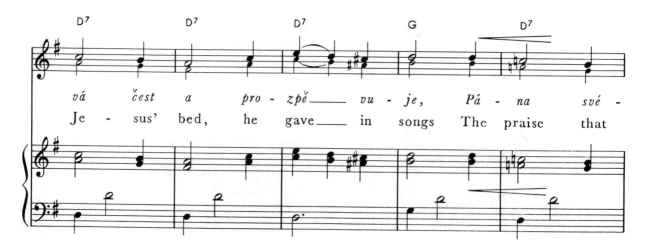

vá čest a pro - zpě — vu - je, Pá - na své -
Je - sus' bed, he gave — in songs The praise that

230

ho vy-chva-lu-je, Ku-ku, ku-ku, ku-ku!
to our God___ be-longs, Cuck-oo, cuck-oo, cuck-oo!

2. *Holoubek sedl na bani,*
   Vkru!
   Dal se silně do houkani,
   Vkru!
   Jest tomu take povděčen,
   Ze jest Ježišek narozen,
   Vkru, vkru, vkru!

2. High in the rafters there sat a dove,
   Coo-roo!
   Cooing to Jesus of his great love,
   Coo-roo!
   His heart and voice so full of joy
   That Heaven sent this lovely Boy!
   Coo-roo, coo-roo, coo-roo!

Sel Bych Rád k Betlému
I GO TO BETHLEHEM

Traditional Czech [GKE]

Traditional Czech [WE]

Ku, ku-ku!   Ku, ku-ku!   Zdráv bu - diz
Coo, coo-coo!   Coo, coo-coo!   Je - sus,   He

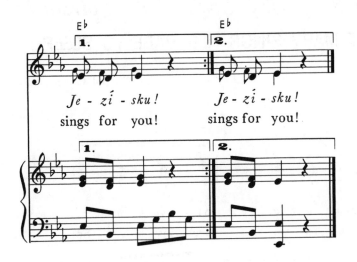

1. Je - zí - sku!   2. Je - zí - sku!
   sings for you!   sings for you!

Chtic, Aby Spal, Tak Zpívala
SWEET MARY SINGS HER BABE TO SLEEP

Traditional Czech [GKE]

Traditional Czech [WE]

Andante sostenuto

1. Chtic, a - by spal tak zpí - va - la   Sy - náč - ko - vi,
1. Sweet Ma - ry sings her Babe to sleep: "Sleep my dear Son,

Mat - ka, jež po - no - co - va - la,   Mi - láč - ko - vi:
While I my lov - ing vig - il keep,   Sleep, dear - est One.

Spi, ne - bes dí - tě mi - lost - né, Pan jsi a Bůh,
An - gels and all of Pa - ra - dise Watch o - ver You;

Pě - je ti v lás - ce ce - lý ráj, Po - zem - ský luh.
E - ven your Fa - ther, God All - Wise, Is watch - ing, too."

2. *Dřimej, to matky zadost je,*
   Holubičko,
   V tobe se duse raduje,
   O perličko!
   Nebesa chvalu peji tvou,
   Slavu a čest,
   Velebi tebe každy tvor,
   Tisice hvezd.

2. "Sweet dreams be with You through the
       night,
   My heav'nly Dove;
   Dream of Your heavenly home so bright,
   My lovely Pearl.
   Thousands of stars together sing,
   Hark to their song!
   They're praising You, their New-Born
       King,
   All the night long."

NESEM VAM NOVINY (KOMMET, IHR HIRTEN) *
COME, HEAR THE WONDERFUL TIDINGS

Traditional Czech [GKE]

Traditional Bohemian-Czech, 1870 [WE]

*The German text for this carol may be found on page 326.

a ne-o-myl-ne, Roz-ji-mej - te.
Come, sing His glo-ry, Je - sus ___ is ___ born!

2. Syna porodila čistá pana,
   V jesličky vložila Krista Pána;
   Jej ovinula a zavinula,
   Jej ovinula a zavinula,
   Plenčičkama.

3. K němužto andělé s nebe přišli,
   I také pastýři jsou se sešli;
   Jeho vítali, Jeho chválili,
   Jeho vítali, Jeho chválili,
   Dary nesli.

4. Anděl Páně jim to sám přikázal,
   Když se jim na poušti všem ukázal:
   K Betlému jiti, neprodlévati,
   K Bethému jiti, neprodlévati,
   Hned přikázal

5. Ejhle, při Kristovu narození
   Stal se div veliký v okamženi:
   Nebo noc tmavá se proměnila,
   Nebo noc tmavá se proměnila,
   V světlo denní.

2. Mary, the sweet Virgin Mother so fine,
   Tenderly comforts the Infant divine;
   Her face is glowing with love o'erflowing,
   Her face is glowing with love o'erflowing,
   For her dear Son.

3. Angels from Heaven are singing His
      praise;
   Shepherds in wonder and joy on Him
      gaze;
   Bringing Him honor, presents they offer,
   Bringing Him honor, presents they offer,
   Jesus, their Lord.

4. Over the desert shines God's radiant star,
   Guiding the kings who come journeying
      far;
   Here to discover, in lowly manger,
   Here to discover, in lowly manger,
   Wisdom divine.

5. Prophecy now is fulfilled in this hour;
   Darkness is scattered by Heaven's great
      pow'r.
   God's glory beaming, o'er Jesus streaming,
   God's glory beaming, o'er Jesus streaming,
   Shines through the night.

237

SUS ÎN POARTA RAIULUI
AT THE GATES OF HEAVEN ABOVE

Traditional Roumanian [GKE]   Traditional Roumanian [WE]

1. Sus în poar - ta rai - u - lui,
1. At the gates of Heav'n a - bove,

Flo - ri - le dal - be sunt de mă - ru,
Ap - ple trees white are bloom - ing sweet - ly,

Flo - ri - le dal - be sunt de măr.
Bloom - ing for Christ, their dear - est love.

238

2. *Sus în poarta raiului,*
   Sade Maica Domnului,
   Sade Maica Domnulu.

3. *Sus în poarta raiului,*
   Fiul plînge, stare n-are,
   Fiul plînge, stare n-ar.

4. *Sus în poarta raiului,*
   Taci fiule, nu mai plînge,
   Taci fiule, nu mai plîng.

5. *Sus în poarta raiului,*
   Două mere, două pere,
   Două mere, două per.

6. *Sus în poarta raiului,*
   Si çheita de la rai,
   Si çheita de la ra.

7. *Sus în poarta raiului,*
   Sa te faci mai mare crai,
   Sa te faci mai mare cra.

2. At the gates of Heav'n above,
   Mary the Mother mild is sitting,
   Holding the Christ, her dearest love

3. At the gates of Heav'n above,
   Her tiny Babe is weeping sadly,
   Weeping is Christ, her dearest love.

4. At the gates of Heav'n above,
   "Hush, my dear Son, I've gifts to give you,
   Gifts for the Christ, my dearest love."

5. At the gates of Heav'n above,
   "Two lovely pears and two fair apples,
   Presents for Christ, my dearest love."

6. At the gates of Heav'n above,
   "Here is the key to Heav'n's portal,
   Open to Christ, my dearest love."

7. At the gates of Heav'n above,
   "Heavenly King to reign forever,
   This is the Christ, my dearest love."

MENYBÖL AR ANGYAL
ANGELS FROM HEAVEN

Traditional Hungarian [GKE]

Traditional Hungarian [WE]

Allegro moderato

1. Meny-böl ar an - gyal le - yött hoz-zá - tok, Pasz - to - rok,
1. An - gels from Heav - en say to the shep-herds, "News we___ bring,

pasz - to - rok; Hogy Bet - le - hem - be si - et - ve men - vén,
news we___ bring! In Beth - le - hem, a - sleep in a man - ger,

Lás - sá - tok, ___ Lás - sá - tok.
Lies your King, ___ Lies your King!"

2. Istennek fia a ki született
Jászolba, jászolba.
O leszen néktek üdvözitötök
Valóban, valóban.

2. "Though born so lowly, yet He is holy,
God's own Son, God's own Son!
He comes to earth to ransom and save you
Ev'ry one, ev'ry one!"

240

ITALIAN CAROLS

Canzone d'i Zampognari

CAROL OF THE BAGPIPERS

Traditional Sicilian
Translation: Dr. Theodore Baker, 1904

Traditional Sicilian [WE]

Andante

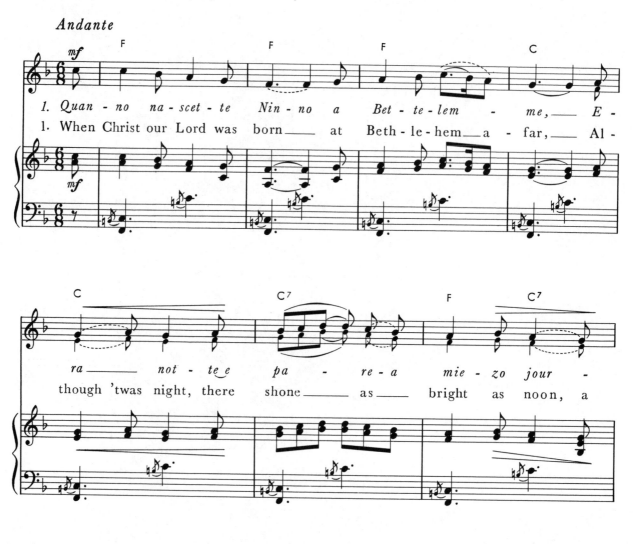

1. Quan - no na - scet - te Nin - no a Bet - te - lem - me,__ E -
1. When Christ our Lord was born__ at Beth - le - hem__ a - far,__ Al -

ra__ not - te e pa - re - a mie - zo jour -
though 'twas night, there shone__ as__ bright as noon, a

no. Ma - je le stel - le, lu - ste - re e bel - le, Se - ve -
star. Nev - er so bright - ly, nev - er so white - ly, Shone__ the

242

det - te - ro ac - cu - sì!   *La chiù lu-cen* ___ *te* ___ *Jet-*
stars, ___ as on ___ that night!   The bright-est star ___ went ___ A

te a chiam-mà li Ma - gi, in O - ri - en - te. ___
way to call the Wise ___ Men ___ from the O - ri - ent. ___

TU SCENDI DALLE STELLE
FROM STARRY SKIES THOU COMEST

Alphonsus Liguori [GKE]

Alphonsus Liguori (1696–1787) [WE]

1. Tu scen - di dal - le stel - le O Re — del Cie -
1. From star - ry skies Thou com - est, The King — of Heav'n fore-

lo ___ E vie - ni in u - na grot - ta Al
told, ___ Ap - pear - ing in a man - ger, Near

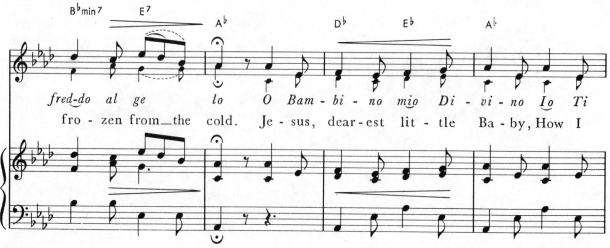

fred - do al ge lo O Bam - bi - no mio Di - vi - no Io Ti
fro - zen from — the cold. Je - sus, dear - est lit - tle Ba - by, How I

ve - do qui tre - mar!_____ O Di - o be - a - to!_____ Oh
long to make Thee warm!_____ To shel - ter Thee_ from harm!_____ My

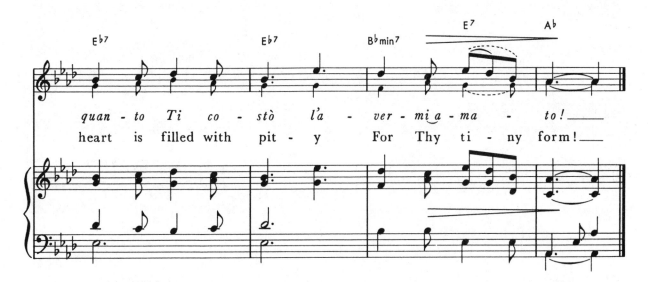

quan - to Ti co - stò l'a - ver - mi a - ma - to!_____
heart is filled with pit - y For Thy ti - ny form!_____

2. *A te, che sei del mondo*
   Il creatore,
   Mancano panni e fuoco,
   O mio Signore.
   Caro, eletto pargoletto,
   Quanto questa poverta
   Piu m'innamora,
   Giacche ti fece amor povero ancora.

2. In Heav'n Thou wert Creator,
   The True and Only Word,
   Yet here on earth no fire, Lord,
   To keep Thee from the cold.
   Jesus, dearest little baby,
   Come in direst poverty,
   Would I had gifts for Thee!
   How wonderful God's love that suffers
     here for me!

Gesù Bambin L'e Nato
JESUS, THE NEW-BORN BABY

Traditional Italian [GKE]

Traditional Italian [WE]

Andante

1. Ge - sù Bam - bin l'e na - to, _____ Na - to in Be - te -

1. Je - sus, the new-born Ba - by, _____ Lies here in Beth - le -

lem _____ L'e so - pra un po' di pa - ia, _____

hem; _____ Born in a hum - ble sta - ble _____

So - pra un po' _____ di fien, _____ L'e so - pra un po' di

Is Heav - en's pre - cious Gem. _____ He is a pre - cious

246

fien S'a j'e'l bam-bin ch'a piu - ra, Soa ma - ma ch'a lo_a -
Gem, Al-though we find Him cry - ing! In Ma-ry's arms He's

do - ra,_____ L'e so - pra un po' di fien._____
sigh - ing,_____ Je - sus, our Di - a - dem._____

2. *Assent na vôs ant l'aira,*
   Assent a vuì ciantand;
   L'è San Giusep so paire
   Lo pija 'ntii so brass!
   S'ai cianta la canssôn,
   Larin, larin, lareta,
   Gloria in Excelsis Deo,
   Tut a l'ônôr 'd l'anfan!

3. We hear a sweet voice singing
   Songs for the Holy One,
   Joseph, the Baby's father,
   Nestles Him close and warm.
   "Loo, loo, my dearest Son."
   O see, 'tis Joseph crooning,
   His tiny Baby soothing!
   Glory to God's own Son!

DORMI, DORMI, O BEL BAMBIN
SLEEP, O SLEEP, MY LOVELY CHILD

Traditional Italian [GKE]

Traditional Italian [WE]

1. Dor - mi, dor - mi, o bel bam - bin, Rè di -
1. Sleep, o sleep, my love - ly Child, King di -

vin, Rè di - vin. Fa la nan - na, o fan - to -
vine, King di - vine. Close Your eyes and sweet - ly

248

li - no,   Rè di - vin,   Rè di - vin.
slum - ber,   King di - vine,   King di - vine.

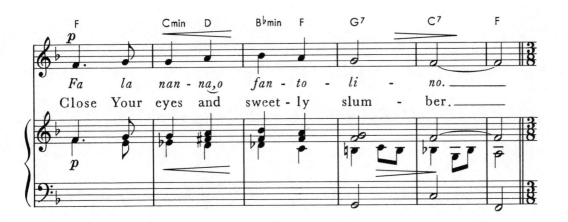

Fa la nan - na,o fan - to - li - no._____
Close Your eyes and sweet - ly slum - ber._____

REFRAIN

Allegro

Fa la la la, Fa la la la la, Fa la
Fa la la la, Fa la la la la, Fa la

2. *Perchè piangi, o mio tresor?*
   Dolce amor, dolce amor!
   Fa la nanna, o caro figlio,
   Tanto bel, tanto bel,
   Fa la nanna, o caro figlio
     Refrain

2. O my treasure, do not weep!
   Sweetly sleep, sweetly sleep,
   Close your eyes my Son, my dear one.
   Sweetly sleep, sweetly sleep.
   Close your eyes, my Son, my dear one.
     Refrain

250

spanish carols

A La Nanita Nana

Traditional Spanish
English lyrics: Norman Luboff

Traditional Spanish Carol [WE]

1. A la na-ni-ta na - na, na-ni-ta e - a, na-ni-ta e - a,

1. A la na-ni-ta na-na na-ni-ta e - a na-ni-ta e - a,

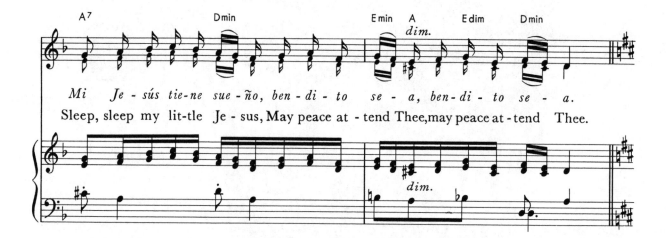

Mi Je-sús tie-ne sue-ño, ben-di-to se - a, ben-di-to se - a.

Sleep, sleep my lit-tle Je - sus, May peace at - tend Thee, may peace at-tend Thee.

Fuen-te-ci - lla que co - rres cla - ra y so - no - ra,

To the world, lit - tle Sav - ior, New hope thou'rt bring - ing

Rui - se - ñor q'en la sel - va can - tan - do llo - ras,
All the world, lit - tle Sav - ior, Thy prais - es sing - ing,

Cal - lad mien-tras la cu - na se ba - lan - ce - a.
God's an-gels hov'-ring o'er Thee chant al - le - lu - ia.

A la na-ni-ta na - na, na-ni - ta e - a.
A la na-ni-ta na - na, na-ni - ta e - a.

253

YA VIENE LA VIEJA
COME, MY DEAR OLD LADY

Traditional Spanish [GKE]   Traditional Spanish [WE]

Allegro

1. Ya vie - ne la vie - ja _____ Con el a - gui -
1. Come, my dear old la - dy, _____ With a lit - tle

nal - do _____ Le pa - re - ce mu - cho, _____
pres - ent _____ That you love so dear - ly, _____

REFRAIN

Le vie - ne qui - tan - do. Pam - pa - ni - tos ver - des, ho - jas de li -
Of - fer it to Je - sus. We're weav - ing a gar - land of green le - mon

254

món, La Vir-gen Ma - ri - a, Ma-dre del Se - ñor.
leaves, For sweet Vir - gin Ma-ry, the Moth-er of God.

2. *Ya vienen los Reyes*
   Por el arenal,
   Y le traen al Niño
   Un torre real.
       Refrain

2. Kings of Orient riding,
   Cross the sandy desert,
   Bringing for the Baby
   Wine and cookies sweet.
       Refrain

3. *Y vienen los Reyes*
   Por aquel camino,
   Y le traen al Niño
   Sopitas en vino
       Refrain

3. Kings of Orient riding,
   Guided by the starlight,
   Bringing to the Baby
   Gifts of love, this night.
       Refrain

LAS POSADAS
THOU ART WELL CONTENT

Traditional Spanish [GKE(adapted)]

Traditional Spanish [WE]

Andante
VERSE

1. Quie - res que te qui - te mi bien de las pa - jas,
1. Thou art well con - tent in a sta - ble so low - ly,

— Quie - res que te_a - do - ren to - dos los pas - to - res.
— Where the shep-herds praise Thee as God's Son so ho - ly.

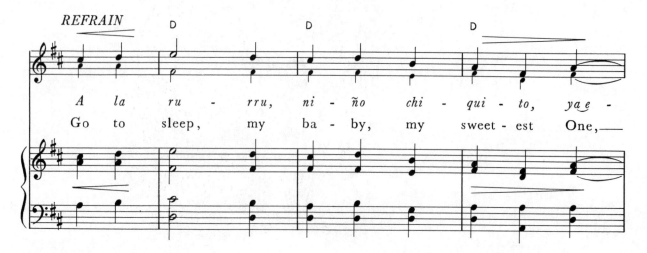

REFRAIN

A la ru - rru, ni - ño chi - qui - to, ya_e -
Go to sleep, my ba - by, my sweet - est One,

staₐarru-lla-di - toₑel ni - ño._____
____ My Je - sus dear,_____ my fair - est._____

2. *Mi querido Padre, mi Dios y Señor*
   Que sufriste alegre del frio su rigor.
   Refrain

2. For Thy dearest Father, the great King of
      Heaven,
   Thou wilt gladly bear any sorrow or
      burden.
         Refrain

Fum, Fum, Fum

FOOM, FOOM, FOOM

Traditional Catalonian Carol [GKE]   Traditional Catalonian Carol [WE]

Allegretto

1. ¡Vein - ti - cin - co   de   di - ciem - bre,   Fum,   fum,   fum!
1. On De - cem - ber   five   and   twen - ty,   Foom,   foom,   foom!

¡Vein - ti - cin - co   de   di - ciem - bre,   Fum,   fum,
On De - cem - ber   five   and   twen - ty,   Foom,   foom,

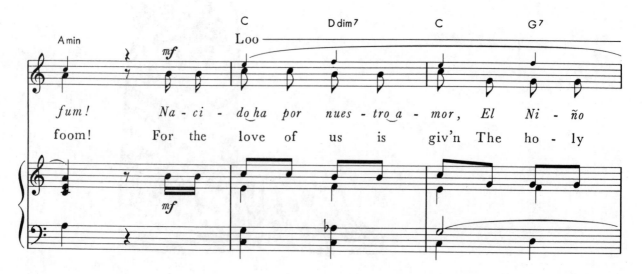

fum!   Na - ci - do ha por   nues - tro a - mor,   El   Ni - ño
foom!   For the   love of   us   is   giv'n   The ho - ly

Dios, el Ni - ño Dios; Hoy de la vir - gen Ma -
In - fant, Son of Heav'n, Of the Vir - gin, Jo - seph's

ri - a En es - ta no - che tan fri - a, ¡Fum, fum, fum!
bride, To all the earth good will be - tid-ing, Foom, foom, foom!

2. ¡Pajaritos de los bosques,
   Fum, fum, fum!
   ¡Pajaritos de los bosques,
   Fum, fum, fum!
   Vuestros hijos de coral
   Abandonad, abandonad,
   Y formad un muelle nido
   A Jesús recién nacido,
   ¡Fum, fum, fum!

2. Little birds from out the forest,
   Foom, foom, foom!
   Little birds from out the forest,
   Foom, foom, foom!
   All your fledglings leave behind,
   And seek the infant Savior kind.
   Come, and build a downy nest
   To warm the lovely Baby blessed,
   Foom, foom, foom!

3. ¡Estrellitas de los cielos,
   Fum, fum, fum!
   ¡Estrellitas de los cielos,
   Fum, fum, fum!
   Que a Jesús mirais llorar
   Y no lloráis, y no lloráis,
   Alumbrad la noche oscura
   Con vuestra luz clara y pura,
   ¡Fum, fum, fum!

3. Little stars up in the heavens,
   Foom, foom, foom!
   Little stars up in the heavens,
   Foom, foom, foom!
   If you see the Baby cry,
   O, do not answer with a sigh!
   Rather, lighten up the sky
   With Heav'n's beams of radiant brightness,
   Foom, foom, foom!

259

El Noi de la Mare
THE SON OF MARY

Traditional Spanish [GKE]

Traditional Catalonian Carol [WE]

Li da - rem fi - gues en un pa - ne - ró. Li da - rem pan - ses en
Then we shall of - fer sweet figs to the Boy. First, we shall give Him a

u - nes ba - lan - ces, Li da - rem fi - gues en un pa - ne - ró.
tray full of rai - sins, Then we shall of - fer sweet figs to the Boy.

2. *Qué li darem al Fillet de Maria,*
   Qué li darem a l'hermós Infantó?
   Panses i figures i nuez i olives,
   Panses i figures i mel i mató.
   Panses i figures i nuez i olives,
   Panses i figures i mel i mató.

2. What shall we give the Beloved of Mary?
   What can we give to her beautiful Child?
   Raisins and olives and nutmeats and
     honey,
   Candy and figs and some cheese that is
     mild.
   Raisins and olives and nutmeats and
     honey,
   Candy and figs and some cheese that is
     mild.

3. *Tam patantam, que les figures son verdes,*
   Tam patantam, que ja madurarán.
   Si no maduren el dia de Pasqua,
   Madurarán en el dia del Ram.
   Si no maduren el dia de Pasqua,
   Madurarán en el dia del Ram.

3. What shall we do if the figs are not
     ripened?
   What shall we do if the figs are still green?
   We shall not fret; if they're not ripe for
     Easter,
   On a Palm Sunday, ripe figs will be seen.
   We shall not fret; if they're not ripe for
     Easter,
   On a Palm Sunday, ripe figs will be seen.

261

Sant Josep i la Mare de Déu
HOLY JOSEPH AND MARY THE MAID

Traditional Catalonian [GKE]

Traditional Catalonian Carol [WE]

1. Sant Jo - sep i la ma - re de Déu___ Fer - en com - pan - yi - a

1. Ho - ly Jo - seph and Ma - ry the maid,___ To whom Christ the Babe was

bo - na,— Par - ti - ren de Nat - za - ret,— Nat - za - ret a la bona
com - ing,— Left be - hind them Na - za - reth,— In the morn - ing's ear - ly

ho - ra. Don do - ron - don, la Ma - re can - ta i el Fil - let dorm.—
dawn - ing."Don do - ron - don," Ma - ry sings— as Je - sus sleeps.—

2. No troben posada enlloo
   De tant que la gent és pobre
   Si no és un barraconet
   Tot ple de joncs i de boga.
   —Don dorondon, la Mare canta i
   el Fillet dorm.

3. Sant Josep va a cercar foc
   A la ciutat i no en troba;
   Quan Sant Josep fou tornat
   Deslliurada en fou l'Esposa
   —Don dorondon, la Mare canta i
   el Fillet dorm.

2. In their poverty, they could not find
   Any room for weary Mary,
   Save a stable, cold and bare;
   'Mid the animals they tarried.
   "Don dorondon," Mary sings as Jesus
   sleeps.

3. Seeking wood, Joseph left Mary there,
   So alone, within the stable;
   To our Lord she then gave birth;
   For a bed, she found a manger.
   "Don dorondon," Mary sings as Jesus
   sleeps.

263

EL REI HERODES
KING HEROD

Traditional Catalonian [GKE]　　　　　　　　　　　　　Traditional Catalonian Carol [WE]

Allegretto

1. Es - tant a la cam - bra Amb— so fill al - mat Re

1. One day Jo - seph, rest - ing, the— Child by his side, Heard

mor va sen - tir - se per— tot la vei - nat. E -

shout - ing and tu - mult that— e - vil be - tide: "The

264

ra el Rei He - ro - des Amb la se - va gent, Que
wick - ed King Her - od has made a de - cree For

fei - a ma - tar___ Tos___ els in - no - cents.
sol - diers to kill ev - 'ry___ in - fant they see."

2. *Anem-se'n Josep,*
   Anem-se'n espós,
   Anem-se'n Egipto
   Sens tenir repós,
   Deixem nostres coses,
   Viandes també,
   Perquó el Rei Herodes
   Diuen que ja ve.

2. "O Joseph, dear husband,
   From here we must go,
   And where we are going,
   No mortal must know.
   Across the wide desert
   To Egypt we'll flee,
   For there, dearest Jesus
   Protected will be."

3. *Amb la somereta*
   Se'n van a cavall
   Seguint les petjades
   Per un cami ral.
   Els angels devallen,
   També els ocellets,
   Perque el bon Jesús
   No fos descobert.

3. Astride of a donkey,
   They hurried along,
   Their pathway was narrow,
   And danger was strong;
   God's angels, and birds,
   Flocking down from the sky,
   The Baby, and Joseph,
   And Mary did hide.

EL DESEMBRE CONGELAT
THE ICY DECEMBER

Traditional Catalonian Carol
Translation: First 2 verses, Anonymous (alt)
Verse 3: [GKE]

Traditional Catalonian Carol [WE]

Andante

1. El de-sem-bre con-ge-lat, Con-fús es re-ti-ra.
1. Cold De-cem-ber's winds were stilled In the month of snow-ing.

A-bril de flors co-ro-nat, Tot el món ad-mi-ra,
As the world fell dark one night, Spring-time's Hope was grow-ing;

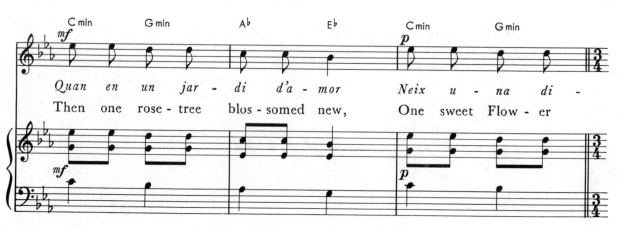

Quan en un jar-di d'a-mor Neix u-na di-
Then one rose-tree blos-somed new, One sweet Flow-er

266

vi - na flor. D'u - na ro ro ro, D'u - na sa sa sa, D'u - na ro, d'u - na
on it grew. On the tree once bare, Grew the Rose so fair, Ah, the Rose, ah, the

sa, D'u - na ro - sa bel - la, Fe - cun - da y pon - cel - la.
Rose, Ah the Rose tree bloom - ing, Sweet the air per - fum - ing.

2. *El primer Pare causá*
   La nit tenevrosa
   Que a tot el mon ofusca
   La vista penosa
   Mes en una mitja nit
   Brilla el sol que n'és eixit
   D'una bel bel bel,
   D'una la la la,
   D'una bel, d'una la,
   D'una bella aurora
   Que el cel enamora.

2. When the darkness fell that night,
   Bringing sweet reposing,
   All the land was hid from sight,
   Sleep our eyes was closing.
   Suddenly, there came a gleam
   From the sky, the wondrous beam
   Of a heav'nly star,
   Giving light afar;
   Ah, the star, ah, the star,
   Ah, the star-beam glowing,
   Brightness ever growing!

3. *El més de maig ha florit,*
   Sense ser encara,
   Un lliri blanc y polit
   De fragáncia rara,
   Que per tot el món se sent,
   De Llevant fins a Ponent,
   Tota sa sa sa
   Tota dul dul dul,
   Tota sa, tota dul,
   Tota sa dulcura
   I olor, amb ventura.

3. Now the month of May was here,
   Filled with God's own radiance;
   Now the purest Lily bloomed,
   Flow'r of sweetest fragrance.
   To the people far and near
   Came a breath of heav'nly cheer;
   O, the incense rare
   Of the Lily there!
   Ah, the scent, ah, the scent
   Of the Lily blooming,
   All the air perfuming!

El Cant dels Ocells
CAROL OF THE BIRDS

Traditional Catalonian [GKE]

Traditional Catalonian Carol [WE]

1. En veu - re des - pun - tar El ma - jor il - lu - mi -

1. Up - on this ho - ly night, When God's great star ap -

nar En la nit més joi - o - sa;

pears, And floods the earth with bright - ness,

268

Els   o - cel - lettes can - tant   a   fes - te - jar - lo
Birds'   voi - ces rise in   song,   And, warb - ling all night

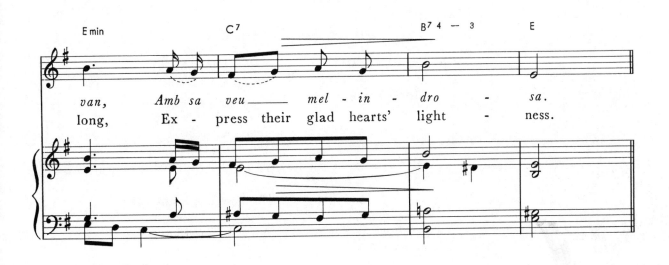

van,   Amb sa   veu   mel - in - dro   - sa.
long,   Ex - press their glad hearts' light   - ness.

Els   o cel - lettes can - tant   A fes - te jar - lo
Birds'   voi - ces rise in   song,   And, warb - ling all night

van ___ Amb sa veu ___ me - lin - dro - sa. ___

long, ___ Ex - press their glad heart's light - ness.

2. *L'ocell rei d'espai*
   Va pels aires volant,
   Cantant amb melodia,
   Dient: — Jesús és nat
   Per treure'ns del pecat
   I darnos alegria.
   Dient: — Jesús és nat
   Per treure'ns del pecat
   I darnos alegria.

3. *Respont-il el pardal:*
   — Esta nit es Nadal
   I es nit de gran contento
   El verdum i el lluer
   Diuen, cantant també:
   — O, quina alegria sento.
   El verdum i el lluer
   Diuen, cantant també:
   —O, quina alegria sento.

4. *Cantava la perdiu:*
   — Me'n vaig a fer el niu
   Dins d'aguella establiam
   Per voure l'Infant
   Com esta tremolant
   En bracos de Maria.
   Per voure l'Infant
   Com esta tremolant
   En bracos de Maria.

2. The Nightingale is first
   To bring his song of cheer,
   And tell us of his glandness:
   "Jesus, our Lord, is born

   To free us from all sin,
   And banish ev'ry sadness!
   Jesus, our Lord, is born
   To free us from all sin,
   And banish ev'ry sadness!"

3. The answ'ring Sparrow cries:
   "God comes to earth this day
   Amid the angels flying."
   Trilling in sweetest tones,
   The Finch his Lord now owns:
   "To Him be all thanksgiving."
   Trilling in sweetest tones,
   The Finch his Lord now owns:
   "To Him be all thanksgiving."

4. The Partridge adds his note:
   "To Bethlehem I'll fly,
   Where in the stall He's lying.
   There, near the manger blest,
   I'll build myself a nest,
   And sing my love undying.
   There, near the manger blest,
   I'll build myself a nest,
   And sing my love undying."

FALADE BEN BAIXO
WE'LL SPEAK VERY SOFTLY

Traditional Galician [GKE]

Traditional Galician Carol [WE]

Sostenuto

1. Fa - la - de ben bai - xo pe - ta - de pou -
1. We'll speak ver - y soft - ly and low - er our

qui - no, Pra que no des - per - te o no - so ro - lli - no, Ay, mi - na
voi - ces Be - fore the dear Sav - ior whom Heav - en re - joi - ces. O my be -

271

xo-ya, meo que-ri-di-no, Eu ben qui-sie-ra dar-che a-go-
lov-ed, could I but hold— Thee, How great my glad-ness, ho-li-est

ri-no, Ter-te no col-lo, a-co-cha-di-no.
rap-ture! How great Thy bless-ing, fall-ing up-on me!

piu mosso

Mi-na xo-ya, meu ra-paz,_____ Mi-na xo-ya,
My be-lov-ed, my heart's_joy, _____ My be-lov-ed,

co - mo es-tás? Que es tás tem - bran - do de fri - o,
how ___ are you? From the cold ___ I see you trem ___ bling,

Ay, que lás - ti - ma me das; Que es - tás tem - bran -
And it grieves me through and through; From the cold ___ I

do de fri - o, Aye, que lás - ti - ma me das.
see you trem - bling, And it grieves me through and through.

OI BETLEHEM
O BETHLEHEM

Traditional Spanish [GKE]

Carol from Biscaya [WE]

1. Oi Bet - le - hem, e - to - ri - da zu -
1. O Beth - le - hem, O'er you a bril - liant

re ga - rai __ a, Oi Bet - le - hem.
star is shin - ing, O Beth - le - hem.

Be - ri - on bat a - die __ raz - ten __
Heav - en - ly choirs of an - gels bring __

274

Bor_____ daz - bor - da da - bil ain - ge - ru - a,
To _____ the world glad news of an in - fant King;

Gaur jai - o de aur - txo Jaun - go - i - ko - a,
Round you the hills _____ and val - leys are e - cho - ing!

Oi Bet - le - hem, _____ Oi Bet - le - hem.
O Beth - le - hem, _____ O Beth - le - hem.

275

EN BELÉN TOCAN A FUEGO
A FIRE IS STARTED IN BETHLEHEM

Traditional Castilian [GKE]

Traditional Castilian Carol [WE]

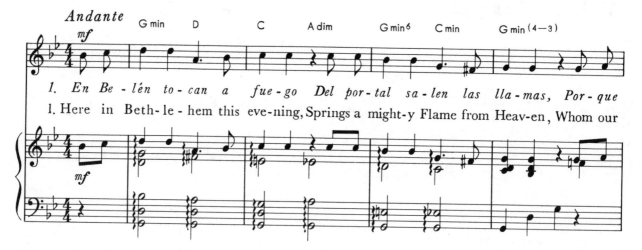

1. En Be - lén to - can a fue - go Del por - tal sa - len las lla - mas, Por - que

1. Here in Beth - le - hem this eve - ning, Springs a might-y Flame from Heav-en, Whom our

di - cen que ha __ na - ci - do El Re - den - tor de las al - mas.

sin - ful-ness will be con - sum - ing, And through Whom we are for - giv - en.

276

Allegro
REFRAIN

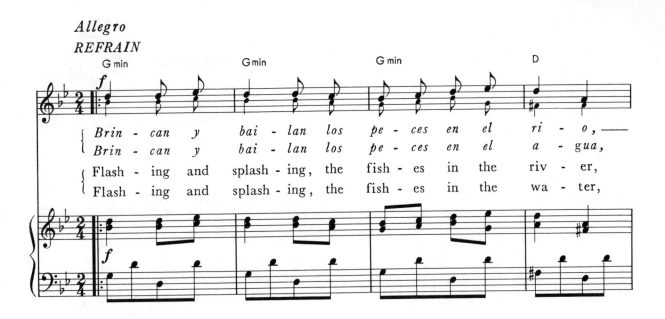

Brin - can y bai - lan los pe - ces en el ri - o, ——
Brin - can y bai - lan los pe - ces en el a - gua,
Flash - ing and splash - ing, the fish - es in the riv - er,
Flash - ing and splash - ing, the fish - es in the wa - ter,

Brin - can y bai - lan de ver a Dios na - ci - do.
Brin - can y bai - lan de ver na - ci - da_el al - ba.
Splash - ing and bow - ing to God, from Heav - en com - ing;
Splash - ing and prais - ing the Light from Heav - en dawn - ing.

2. *En el portal de Belén*
   Nació_un clavel encarnado
   Que por redimir el mundo
   Se_ha vuelto lirio morado.
        Refrain

2. In a cold and humble stable,
   Blooms a spotless white Carnation,
   That becomes a lovely purple Lily,
   Sacrificed for our redemption.
        Refrain

3. *La Virgen lava panales*
   Y los tiende_en el romero,
   Los pajarillos cantaban
   Y el agua se_iba riendo.
        Refrain

3. Washing swaddling clothes for Jesus,
   Mary by a stream is singing.
   Birdlings chirp to her a joyful greeting,
   And the rippling brook is laughing.
        Refrain

Campana Sobre Campana
BELLS OVER BETHLEHEM

Traditional Andalucian [GKE]   Traditional Andalucian Carol [WE]

Allegro

1.¡Cam-pa-na so-bre cam-pa - na   Cam-pa-na so-bre cam-pa - na!
1.Bells o-ver Beth-le-hem peal - ing,   God's sa-cred pres-ence re - veal - ing!

A - só-ma-te a la ven-ta - na   Ver - as a un Ni-ño en la   cu - na.
There in a cra-dle is   rest - ing   Je - sus, the earth's rich-est bless - ing!

REFRAIN

"Be - lén, cam-pa-nas de Be - lén, Qué los an-ge-les to-can Que nue-vas me tra-óis?"
The bells, the bells of Beth-le - hem Are ring-ing out the ti-dings, "good will __ to all men!"

278

Re - co - gi - do tu re - ba - no A dón-de vas pas - tor-ci - to___
Leave your sheep_ and come, O shep-herds, pres - ents bring the Babe so low - ly, ___

Voy a lle - var al por-tal___ Re - que-són, man te - ca y vi - no. "Be-
Bring some cheese and bring some wine ___ For the Moth - er Ma - ry ho - ly. The

lén, cam-pa-nas de Be - lén, Qué los an - ge - les to - can, Qué nue-vas me tra - ois?"
bells, the bells of Beth-le - hem Are ring-ing out the ti-dings, "Good will ___ to all men!"

2. *Si aun las estrellas alumbran,*
   Pastor, dónde quieres ir?
   —Voy al portal por si el Niño
   Con El me deja dormir.
   Refrain

2. Shepherds, if you will but hasten,
   Mary the beautiful Virgin,
   May grant that you may be keeping
   Watch o'er the dear Baby sleeping.
   Refrain

Chiquirriquitin
O MY LOVELIEST ONE

Traditional Spanish [GKE]

Traditional Andalucian [WE]

tin,} chi-qui-rri-qui-tin, {Que-re-di, que-re-di-to del al - ma."
One,}   To my heart You must not be a stran - ger!"

tin, _____ Que-re-di, que-re-di-to del al - ma."
One, _____ To my heart You must not be a stran - ger!"

VERSE

Slower

Por de-ba-jo del ar - co Del por-ta-li - ño,
See the won-der-ful vi - sion Here in a sta - ble,

Se des-cu-bre a Ma - ri - a, Jo-se, y el Ni - ño.
Jo - seph, sweet Vir - gin Ma - ry, and Heav - en's Ba - by.

2. *Entre el buey y la mula*
   Dios ha nacido
   Y en un pobre pesebre
   lo han recogido
   Refrain

2. 'Twixt the ass and the oxen
   Jesus is lying;
   In a cradle so humble,
   God's Love undying!
   Refrain

281

En el Portal a Belén
IN BETHLEHEM'S CRADLE

Traditional Puerto Rican [GKE]

Traditional Puerto Rican [WE]

1. Ha na - ci - do en un por - tal — Lle-ni - to de te - la - ra-ñas, En-tre
1. He is born with-in a sta-ble, In the bit-ter cold of win-ter; 'Twixt the

la mu - la y el bu - ey, El Re - den - tor de las al - mas.
ox and ass He's ly-ing, Heav-en's Babe, the world's re - deem-er.

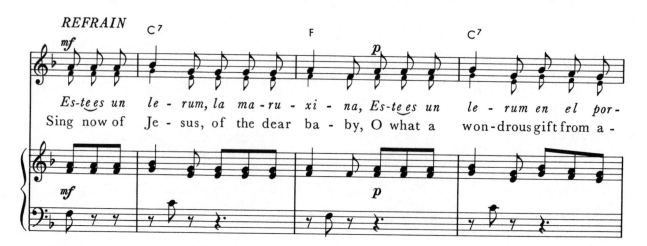

Es-te es un le - rum, la ma-ru - xi - na, Es-te es un le - rum en el por-
Sing now of Je - sus, of the dear ba - by, O what a won-drous gift from a-

282

tal; Va-ya pro-si-go es-te can-tar, Va-ya pro-si-go es-te can-
bove! He has our hearts and all of our love! He has our hearts and all of our

tar. ⎫ Le - rum, le - rum, le - rum, la! (¡Que vi - va!)
love! ⎭

2. En el portal de Belén
   Hay estrella, sol y luna:
   La Virgen y San José
   Y el Niño que está en la cuna
   Refrain

2. There within the dingy stable
   Sun and moon and star are shining:
   Joseph, Mary and the Baby,
   For whom all our hearts were pining.
   Refrain

3. Entró al portal un gallego
   Que vengo desde Galicia
   Y le traigo al Niño Diós
   Lienzo para una camisa
   Refrain

3. To His side, a lowly shepherd,
   From the Spanish plains appearing,
   Brings the Baby gifts of linen,
   So a shirt He can be wearing.
   Refrain

4. Entró un gitano al portal
   De Granada vengo a aqui
   Y le traigo al Niño Diós
   Un gallo quiquiriqui.
   Refrain

4. Also near Him stands a gypsy
   From Granada he comes hieing,
   Bringing to the Babe a rooster;
   "Cock-a-doodle-doo," it's crying.
   Refrain

283

EL SANTO NIÑO
THE HOLY CHILD

Traditional Puerto Rican [GKE]

Traditional Puerto Rican [WE]

Andante

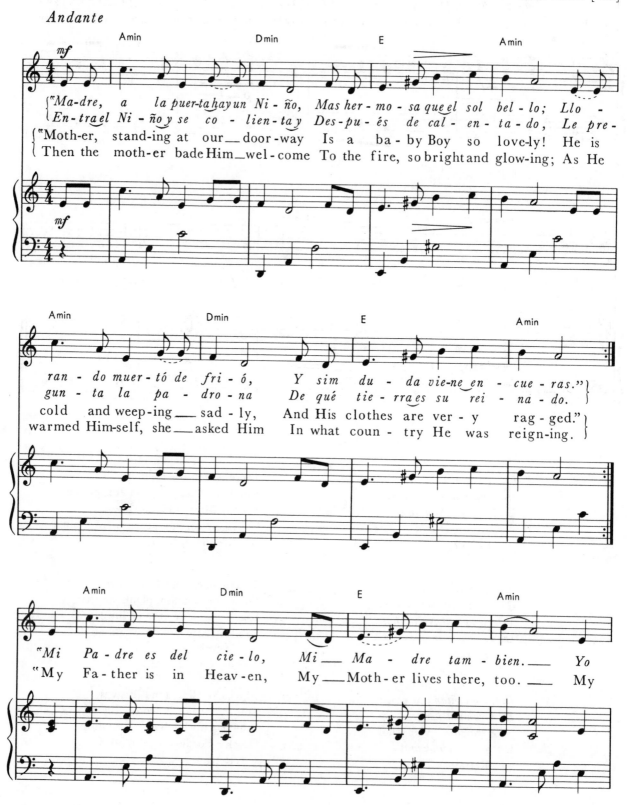

{"Ma-dre, a la puer-ta hay un Ni - ño, Mas her - mo-sa que el sol bel - lo; Llo -
{En-tra el Ni - ño y se co - lien-ta y Des-pu - és de cal - en-ta-do, Le pre -

{"Moth-er, stand-ing at our__ door-way Is a ba - by Boy so love-ly! He is
{Then the moth-er bade Him__ wel-come To the fire, so bright and glow-ing; As He

ran - do muer-tó de fri - ó, Y sim du - da vie-ne en - cue - ras."}
gun - ta la pa - dro - na De qué tie - rra es su rei - na - do. }

cold and weep-ing__ sad - ly, And His clothes are ver - y rag - ged."}
warmed Him-self, she__ asked Him In what coun - try He was reign-ing. }

"Mi Pa - dre es del cie - lo, Mi__ Ma - dre tam - bien.__ Yo
"My Fa - ther is in Heav - en, My__ Moth - er lives there, too.__ My

284

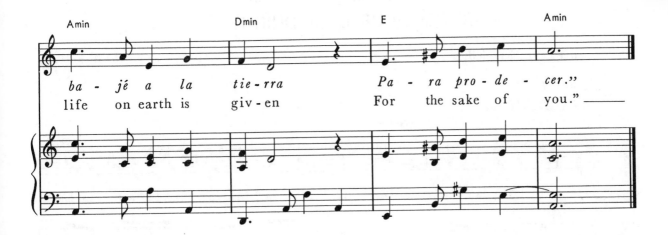

ba - jé a la tie - rra   Pa - ra pro - de - cer."
life   on earth is   giv - en   For   the sake of   you." _____

A la Media Noche
AT THE HOUR OF MIDNIGHT

Traditional Puerto Rican [GKE]

Traditional Puerto Rican [WE]

Allegretto
INTRODUCTION

La la la la la la la la, La la la la la la la la la la la, La

la la la la la la la, La la la la la la. La la.

A la me - dia no - che ___ al ri - gor del hie - lo ___
At the hour of mid - night, ___ in the midst of win - ter, ___

286

2. *Entre pajas nace del cielo gran Rey*
   A su lado tiene la mula y el buey.
   El buey como humilde las pajas le echaba
   La maldita mula le descobijaba.

2. Heaven's King eternal on the straw is lying.
   Mule and ox stand near Him; from the cold He's crying.
   Spreading hay to warm Him, ox o'er Jesus hovers;
   But the mule is wicked—he the Babe uncovers.

3. *Su madre lo mira sin poderle dar*
   Ni lecho ni cuna donde reposar
   Tiernecito Niño, mi Jesús, mi Diós
   Eres suave y dulce, eres todo amor.

3. Mary weeps in pity for her suff'ring darling,
   Wishing for protection from the cold winds howling.
   "Tend'rest little infant Savior, O my Jesus,
   All my love forever, sweetest Son so precious."

SONG OF THE WISE MEN

Traditional Puerto Rican [GKE]

Traditional Puerto Rican [WE]

Andante con moto

VERSE

1. De tie-rra le - ja - na Ve - ni-mos a ver - te,
1. From a dis - tant home, The Sav-ior we come seek - ing,

Nos sir-ve de gui - a La Es-tre - lla de O - rien - te.
Us-ing as our guide the star, so bright-ly beam - ing.

REFRAIN

O bri - llan - te es - tre - lla que a-nun - cias la au -
Glo-ria en las al - tu - ras al Hi - jo de
Love - ly East - ern Star, that tells us of God's
Glo - ry in the High - est to the Son of

288

A7

ro - ra   No nos fal - te nun - ca tu luz bien-he -
Di - os,   Glo-ria en las al - tu - ras
morn - ing,   Heav-en's won-drous light,   O nev-er cease Thy
Hea - ven,   And up-on the earth   be

1.

Dmin   A7   Dmin   Dmin

2.

cho - ra.   y en la tie - rra a - mor. ____
shin - ing!   peace and love to men. ____

2. *Al recién nacido que es Rey de los reyes,*
   Oro le regalo para ornar sus sienes.

2. Glowing gold I bring to the new-born
      Babe so holy,
   Token of His pow'r to reign above in
      glory.

3. *Como es Diós el Niño le regalo incienso,*
   Perfume con alma que sube hasta el
      cielo.

3. Frankincense I bring to the Child of God's
      own choosing,
   Token of our pray'rs to Heaven ever
      rising.

4. *Al Niño del cielo que bajó a la tierra,*
   Le regalo mirra que inspira tristeza.

4. Bitter myrrh have I to give the infant
      Jesus,
   Token of the pain that He will bear to
      save us.

PASTORES A BELÉN
SHEPHERDS IN BETHLEHEM

Traditional Puerto Rican [GKE]

Traditional Puerto Rican [WE]

1. Pas - to - res a Be - lén___ va - mos con a - le - gri - a, Que

1. The Lord to earth has come,___ ap - pear - ing as__ a Ba - by, He

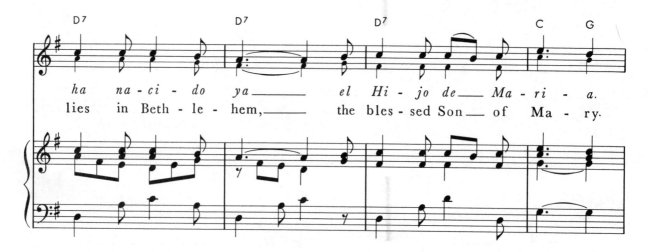

ha na - ci - do ya___ el Hi - jo de___ Ma - ri - a.

lies in Beth - le - hem,___ the bles - sed Son___ of Ma - ry.

A - llí,___ a - llí,___ Nos es - pe - ra Je - sús.___

A - llí,___ a - llí,___ Nos es - pe - ra Je - sús.___

O come,___ O come,___ O shep - herds, run to see,___

The Ho - ly Babe___ That brings us Heav - en's peace.___

290

Lle - ve - mos pues tu - rro-nes y miel Pa - ra of-re-cer al Ni - ño Man-uel, Lle -
Come car - ry-ing some nuts and some hon-ey, Of - fer them to Je-sus to eat, Come

ve - mos pues tu - pro-nes y miel Pa - ra of-re-cer al Ni - ño Man-uel.
car - ry-ing some nuts and some hon - ey, Of - fer them to Je-sus to eat.

Va - mos, va - mos, va - mos a ver, Va - mos a ver al
Has - ten, has - ten, haste to a - dore! Je - sus is born, the

291

re - cien na - ci - do, Va - mos a ver al Ni - ño Man - uel.
Son of the High - est, Je - sus our King, for - ev - er - more.

Alegría

HAPPILY SINGING

Traditional Puerto Rican [GKE]　　　　　　　　　　　Traditional Puerto Rican [WE]

1. Ha-cia Be-lén___ se en-ca - mi-nan___ Ma-ría con su a - man-te es-
1. On the road-way___ to the cit - y,___ rides the Vir-gin___ on a

po - so;___ Lle - van - do en su___ com-pa - ñí - a___ Un to-
don - key;___ Trav-'ling with her___ and dear Jo - seph___ is God's

do un Dios ___ po - de - ro-so___ A - le - grí - a, a - le - grí - a, a - le -
Spir - it___ so al - might-y___ We are hap-pi - ly, hap-pi - ly

293

grí - a,_____ A - le - grí-a,a-le-grí-a y pla - cer_____ Que la
sing - ing,_____ Let-ting mel-o-dy joy-ful-ly ring,_____ For sweet

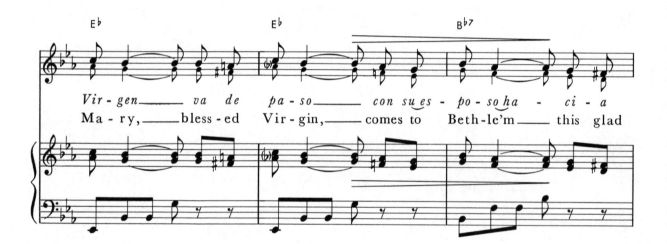

Vir - gen_____ va de pa - so_____ con su es-po-so ha - ci - a
Ma - ry,_____ bless-ed Vir - gin,_____ comes to Beth-le'm_____ this glad

Be - lén;_____ A - le - grí-a,a-le-grí-a,a-le - grí-a_____ A - le -
eve-ning;_____ We are hap-pi-ly, hap-pi-ly sing-ing,_____ Let-ting

294

grí - a, a - le - grí - a y pla - cer_____ Que la Vir - gen_____ va de
mel - o - dy joy - ful - ly ring, _____ For sweet Ma - ry, _____ bless - ed

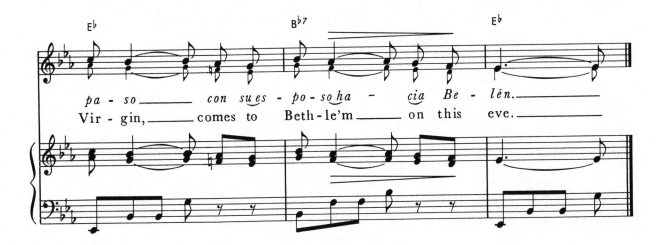

pa - so_____ con su es - po - so ha - cia Be - lén. _____
Vir - gin, _____ comes to Beth - le'm _____ on this eve. _____

2. *En cuanto a Belén llegaron*
   Posada al punto pidieron,
   Nadie les quiso hospedar
   Porque tan pobres les vieron.
      Refrain

3. *Los pajarillos del bosque*
   Al ver pasar los esposos,
   Le cantaban melodías
   Con sus trinos armoniosos.
      Refrain

2. *In the evening, on arriving*
   In the noisy, crowded city,
   There is no place to find lodging
   For the Virgin, weak and weary.
      Refrain

3. From the forest, birds come winging,
   To the city they come streaming,
   Sweetest music they are trilling,
   Frightened Mary to be cheering.
      Refrain

Cantemos
WE ARE SINGING

Traditional Venezuelan [GKE]

Venezuelan Folk Carol [WE]

Andante
REFRAIN

1. Can-te-mos, can-te-mos Glo-ria al Sal-va-dor.
1. Sing-ing, we are sing-ing! Lov-ing praise we bring:

Fe-liz No-che-bue-na, Fe-liz No-che-bue-na
Hap-py Eve of Christ-mas, Hap-py Eve of Christ-mas,

Fe-liz No-che-bue-na Nos dé el Ni-ño Dios,____
Hap-py Eve of Christ-mas, To Thee, In-fant King.____

Fine

VERSE

Tú er-es la es-pe - ran - za, Tú la ca - ri - dad,___
All our ex-pec - ta - tion, All our char-i - ty,___

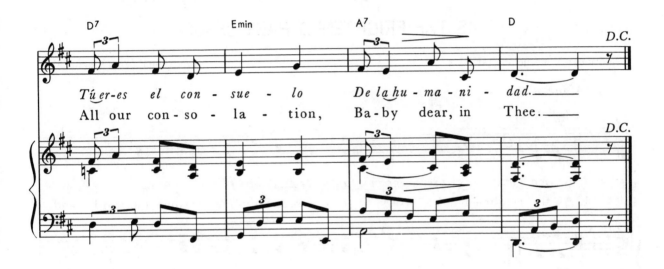

Tú er-es el con - sue - lo De la hu - ma - ni - dad.___
All our con-so - la - tion, Ba-by dear, in Thee.___

D.C.

2. *Divinos destellos*
   Raudales de luz,
   Alumbran la cuna
   Del Niño Jesús
   Refrain

2. Beaming through the darkness,
   Flooding rays so bright,
   Shining on the cradle,
   Coming from on High.
   Refrain

3. *O noche dichosa,*
   Noche de esplendor,
   Noche en que ha nacido
   Nuestro Redentor.
   Refrain

3. Night of jubilation
   Night of Jesus' birth,
   Night of holy splendor,
   And redeeming love.
   Refrain

297

Como Busca el Tierno Infante
AS THE FRIGHTENED BABY JESUS

Traditional Venezuelan [GKE]

Traditional Venezuelan [WE]

Moderato

1. Co-mo bus-ca el tier-no in-fan - te___ A-fli - gi-do y pe - sa-
1. As the fright-ened ba - by Je - sus,___ Shiv-'ring from the cold and

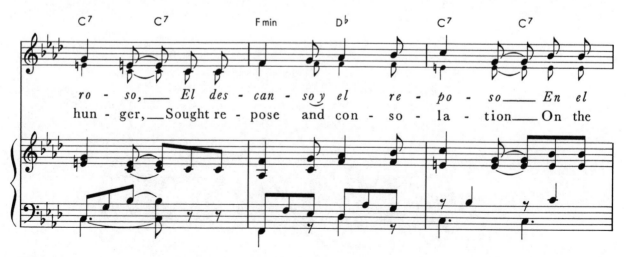

ro - so,___ El des - can - so y el re - po - so___ En el
hun - ger,___ Sought re - pose and con - so - la - tion___ On the

298

se - no ma - ter - nal,   A - si yo, des - de que
Vir - gin Moth - er's breast;   So would I,   as day is

bri - lla   Le blan - ca   luz de la au - ro - ra,   Ven - go a
dawn - ing,   Come to Thee,   O Ho - ly Ma - ry,   Seek - ing

bus - car, O Señ - o - ra, Tu pro - tec - ción ce - les - tial.____
Thy blest con - so - la - tion, And to pray for heav'n-ly rest.____

LA JORNADA
THE JOURNEY

Traditional Venezuelan [GKE]

Venezuelan Folk Carol [WE]

Allegro
REFRAIN

1. *Din, din, din, Es ho-ra de par-tir,*
1. Din, din, din, We must be on our way,

Din, din, din. Ca-mi-no de Be-lén.
Din, din, din, Be-fore the break of day.

Los es-po-sos van_____ des de Na-za-ret,
Length-y is the jour-ney to reach Beth-le-hem,

Los es-po-sos van_____ des de Na-za-ret.
Length-y is the jour-ney to reach Beth-le-hem.

VERSE

La Vir - gen Ma - rí - a,
Dear-est Vir - gin Ma - ry,

Mo-des-ta y sen - ci - lla, Es la ma-ra-vi - lla
Shy and or-di-na - ry, You bring great-est hope and

301

Del di - cho - so E - den
Joy to Par - a - dise!

Del di - cho - so E - den.
Joy to Par - a - dise.

2. *Sobre un jumentillo*
   Se sienta María
   Y es experto guia
   El castro José.
       Refrain

2. Seated on a donkey,
     Mary now was ready;
     Joseph would be guiding,
     Walking all the way.
       Refrain

3. *Los buenos amigos*
   De José y María
   Llegan a porfía
   A decirle adiós.
       Refrain

3. Wishing God's protection,
     Friends were gathered 'round them,
     Clasping hands in blessing,
     Watching them depart.
       Refrain

4. *Largo es el camino;*
   Aire sofocante;
   Mas es importante
   Cumplir el deber.
       Refrain

4. O, how long the road was!
     And how hot the air was!
     But they both must bear it,
     For it was God's will.
       Refrain

5. *Llegan extenuados*
   Al morir el día,
   Y en la noche fría
   No hay donde hospedar
       Refrain

5. Daylight's rays were dying
     Ere they were arriving,
     But they found no lodging
     In night's growing cold.
       Refrain

6. *José solicita,*
   Fuerte y animoso,
   Lugar de reposo
   En todo Belén.
       Refrain

6. Joseph begged and pleaded,
     But he was not heeded;
     Not a door was open
     In all Bethlehem.
       Refrain

7. *Posadas repletas*
   De inmenso gentío;
   ¡Ah, Señor, Dios mio!
   ¿A donde llegar?
       Refrain

7. "Ev'ry road we travel,
     Crowded full of people!
     Where, O heav'nly Father,
     Can we shelter find?"
       Refrain

8. *Y saliendo al campo*
   Una gruta encuentran
   Y en ella se adentran
   Para pernoctar.
       Refrain

8. Trudging through a meadow,
     Stumbling on a grotto,
     Joseph led poor Mary
     Inside for the night.
       Refrain

Vamos a Belén
GOING TO BETHLEHEM

Traditional Chilean [GKE]

Traditional Chilean Carol [WE]

1. Bue - nas no - ches, Ma - ri - qui - ta,____ Yo ven - go con mu - cho
1. Good eve - ning, dear lit - tle Ma - ry,____ My heart is filled with much

pe - na,____ Yo ven - go con mu - cho pe - na;____ Por -
pit - y,____ My heart is filled with much pit - y;____ For

que al Ni - ñi - to Je - sús,____ Se le a - ca - bo la no -
you and Je - sus so love - ly,____ A fer - vent pray'r I am

ve - na._____ Se le a - ca - bo la no - ve - na.
giv - ing,_____ A fer - vent pray'r I am giv - ing.

Va - mos, va - mos, va - mos, a Be - lén,____ Va - mos, va - mos que va - mos a
Go - ing, go - ing, to Beth - le - hem town,____ Go - ing, go - ing the Ba - by to

ver,_____ A ver al Ni - ño Je - sús,_____ La
see,_____ To greet his fa - ther, Jo - seph,_____ And

Virgen y San Je - sé.
Ma - ry, Vir-gin so sweet.

Vir - gen y San Jo - sé.
Ma - ry, Vir-gin so sweet.

2. *Adiós, mi buen Manuelito,*
   Hasta el año venidero,
   Hasta el año venidero;
   Nos volveremos a ver
   Cuando engorden los corderos,
   Cuando engorden los corderos.
   Refrain

3. *Señora doña Maria*
   Macetita de azucena,
   Macetita de azucena;
   Le daré la despedida
   Esta noche es Nochebuena,
   Esta noche es Nochebuena.
   Refrain

2. Goodbye to you, little Manuel,
   Until the New Year is breaking,
   Until the New Year is breaking;
   I'll see you after the shearing,
   So rich from wool you'll be selling,
   So rich from wool you'll be selling!
   Refrain

3. O Mary, Holiest Mother,
   As pure as lilies unfolding,
   As pure as lilies unfolding;
   I come on this eve of Christmas,
   Thy love and glory beholding,
   Thy love and glory beholding.
   Refrain

En Nombre del Cielo

PRAY GIVE US LODGING

Traditional Mexican [GKE] Traditional Mexican Carol [WE]

Allegretto

1. San José: En____ nom - bre____ del cie - - - lo,
1. Joseph. Pray give us lodg - ing dear, sir, in the name of Heav'n!

Os - pi - do____ po - sa - - da
All day since morn - ing to tra - vel__we've__ giv'n,

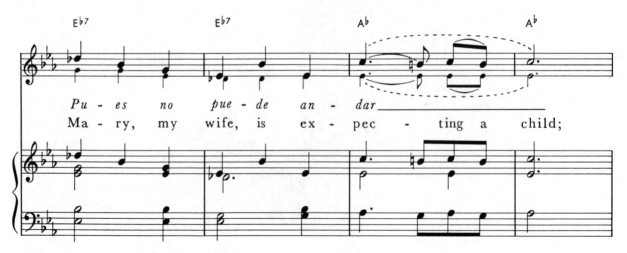

Pu - es no pue - de an - dar____
Ma - ry, my wife, is ex - pec - ting a child;

306

Mi____ es - po - sa a - ma - - - - da.
She must have shel - ter to - night. Let__ us__ in, let__ us __ in!

2. *Huésped: Aquí no es mesón*
   Sigan adelante
   Yo no puedo abrir
   No sea algún tunante.

2. Host: You cannot stop here, I won't
   make my house an inn;
   I do not trust you, your story is
   thin.
   You two might rob me and then
   run away—
   Find somewhere else you can stay.
   Go away! go away!

3. *San José: No seas inhumano;*
   Tennos caridad.
   Que el Dios de los cielos
   Te lo premiará

3. Joseph: Please show us pity! Your heart
   cannot be this hard!
   Look at poor Mary, so worn and
   so tired!
   We are most poor, but I'll pay
   what I can;
   God will reward you, good man!
   Let us in! let us in!

4. *Huésped: Ya se pueden ir*
   Y no molestar.
   Porque si me enfado
   Los voy a apalear.

4. Host: You try my patience! I'm tired and
   must get some rest;
   I've told you nicely, but still you
   insist.
   If you don't go and stop bothering
   me,
   I'll fix you, I guarantee!
   Go away! go away!

5. *San José: Mi esposa es María*
   Es Reina del Cielo,
   Y madre va a ser
   Del Divino Verbo.

5. Joseph: Sir, I must tell you, my wife is
   the Queen of Heaven,
   Chosen by God to deliver his Son.
   Jesus is coming to earth on this
   eve;
   (O Heaven, make him believe!)
   Let us in! let us in!

6. *Huésped: ¿Eres tú José?*
   ¿Tu esposa es María?
   Entren, peregrinos,
   No los conocía.

6. Host: Joseph, dear Joseph! O how could
   I be so blind?
   Not to know you and the Virgin so
   fine!
   Enter, blest pilgrims, my house is
   your own;
   Praise be to God on His throne!
   Please come in! please come in!

El Rorro
THE BABE

Traditional Mexican [GKE]

Mexican Lullaby Carol [WE]

Andante

REFRAIN

1. A la ru - ru - ru, ni-ño chi - qui - to, Duer-ma-se ya____ mi Je - su-

1. A la ru - ru - ru, My love-ly Je - sus, In sweet-est slum - ber now rest, my

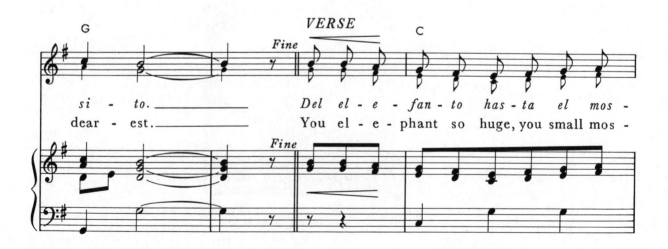

VERSE

si - to.____

dear - est.____

Del el - e - fan - to has - ta el mos-

You el - e - phant so huge, you small mos-

qui - to, Guar-den si - len-cio, no le ha-gan ru - i - do.
qui - to, Be ver-y still, you must not wake the Ni - ño.*

* Baby

2. *Noche venturosa, noche de alegria.*
   Bendita la dulce, divina Maria.
   Refrain

2. O night of glory, night of jubilation,
   So richly blest by Mary, Queen of Heaven.
   Refrain

3. *Coros celestiales, con su dulce accento,*
   Canten la ventura de este nacimiento
   Refrain

3. Such heav'nly voices in sweet accents
   singing,
   The glorious tidings of His birth are
   bringing!
   Refrain

VAMOS, PASTORCITOS

HASTEN NOW, O SHEPHERDS

Traditional Colombian [GKE]

Colombian Carol [WE]

1. ¡Va-mos, pas - tor-ci - tos, Va-mos a Be - lén!
1. Has-ten now, O shep-herds, Go to Beth - le - hem!

A ver a la Vir - gen y Al Ni - no tam - bién.
There to see the Vir - gin And her in - fant Son.

2. *Al pequeño Niño*
   Que ha nacido ya,
   Con alegres cantos
   Vamos a arrullar.

2. Such a tiny Infant,
   Born this holy day!
   Cheer Him with your singing
   Of a lullaby.

3. *Vamos, pastorcitos,*
   Vamos a adorar
   La Rey de los cielos
   Que está en el portal.

3. Hasten now, O shepherds,
   Hasten to adore
   Jesus, gift of Heaven,
   King forevermore!

310

LATIN CAROLS

VENI, EMMANUEL

O COME, O COME, EMMANUEL

9th Century Latin
Published in Cologne, 1710
Translation: John M. Neale, 1818–1866

13th Century Plainsong
Adapted by Thomas Helmore, 1854
Arrangement: [WE]

Andante con moto

1. Ve - ni, ve - ni Em - ma - nu -
1. O come, O come, Em - man - u -

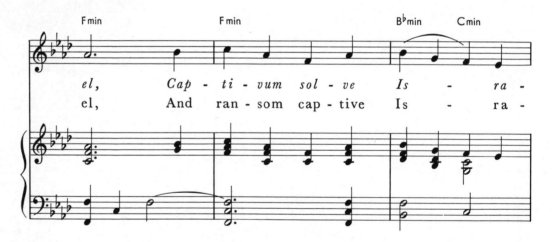

el, Cap - ti - vum sol - ve Is - ra -
el, And ran - som cap - tive Is - ra -

el, Qui ge - mit in ex - i - li -
el, That mourns in lone - ly ex - ile

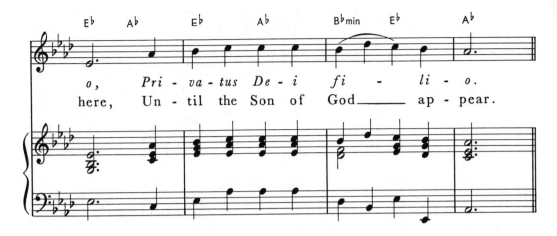

o, *Pri - va - tus De - i fi - li - o.*
here, Un - til the Son of God___ ap - pear.

REFRAIN

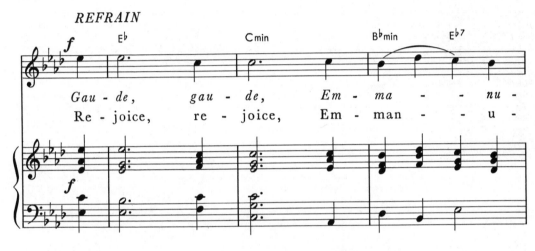

Gau - de,   gau - de,   Em - ma - - nu -
Re - joice,   re - joice,   Em - man - - u -

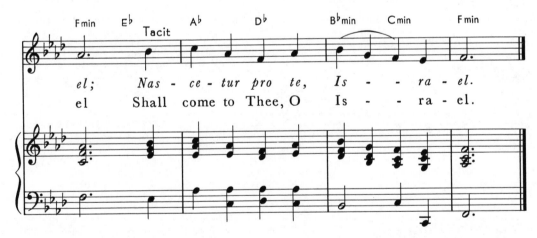

el;   Nas - ce - tur pro te,   Is - - ra - el.
el   Shall   come to Thee, O   Is - - ra - el.

2. *Veni, veni, O Oriens,*
   Solare nos adveniens:
   Noctis despelle nebulas,
   Dirasque noctis tenebras.
        Refrain

2. O come, Thou Dayspring, come and cheer
   Our spirits by Thine advent here;
   Disperse the gloomy clouds of night,
   And death's dark shadows put to flight.
        Refrain

3. *Veni, clavis Davidica,*
   Regna reclude caelica,
   Fac iter tutum superum,
   Et claude vias inferum.
        Refrain

3. O come, Thou Key of David, come,
   And open wide our heav'nly home;
   Make safe the way that leads on high,
   And close the path to misery.
        Refrain

313

Corde Natus Ex Parentis

OF THE FATHER'S LOVE BEGOTTEN

Aurelius Clemens Prudentius, 348–413
Translation: John M. Neale, 1854

Trope to a 13th Century Sanctus [WE]

Andante

1. Cor - de na - tus ex pa - ren - tis, An - te mun - di ex - or - di - um
1. Of the Fa-ther's love be-got - ten, Ere the worlds be - gan___ to be,

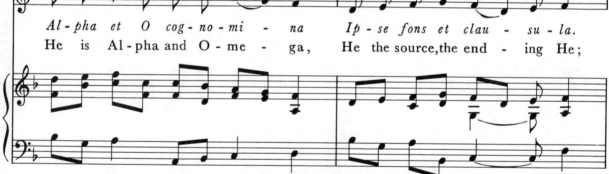

Al - pha et O cog - no - mi - na Ip - se fons et clau - su - la.
He is Al - pha and O - me - ga, He the source, the end - ing He;

Om - ni - um quae sunt fu - e - - runt, Quae que
Of the things that are, that have_____ been, And that

post fu - tu - ra sunt, Sae - cu - lo - rum se - cu - la._____

fu - ture years shall see, Ev - er - more and ev - er - more!_____

2. *O beatus ortus ille,*
   Virgo cum puerpera
   Edidit nostram salutem,
   Feta sancto Spiritu,
   Et puer, redemptor orbis,
   Os sacratum protulit,
   Saeculorum saeculis.

2. O that birth forever blessed,
   When the Virgin, full of grace,
   By the Holy Ghost conceiving,
   Bore the Savior of our race;
   And the Babe, the world's Redeemer,
   First revealed His sacred face,
   Evermore and evermore!

3. *Psallit altitudo caeli,*
   Psallant omnes angeli:
   Quidquid est virtutis usquam
   Psallat in laudem Dei:
   Nulla linguarum silescat,
   Vox et omnis consonet,
   Saeculorum saeculis.

3. O ye heights of Heav'n, adore Him;
   Angel hosts, His praises sing;
   Pow'rs, dominions, bow before Him,
   And extol our God and King;
   Let no tongue on earth be silent,
   Ev'ry voice in concert ring,
   Evermore and evermore!

Puer Natus in Bethlehem
A BOY IS BORN IN BETHLEHEM

Traditional Latin [GKE]

14th Century Latin Carol [WE]

Allegretto

1. Pu - er na - tus in Beth - le - hem, Al - le -
1. A Boy is born in Beth - le - hem, Al - le -

lu - ja! Un - de gau - det Je - ru - sa -
lu - ja! And joy is in Je - ru - sa -

lem, Al - lu - lu - ia, Al - le - lu - ia!
lem, Al - le - lu - ja, Al - le - lu - ja!

2. *Per Gabrielem nuntiam*
   Virgo concepit Filium.

3. *Reges de Saba veniunt,*
   Aurum, thus, myrrham offerunt.

4. *Laudetur sancta Trinitas,*
   Deo dicamus gratias.

2. Through Gabriel, Heav'ns appointed one,
   The Virgin bears a holy Son.

3. The wisest kings of Orient
   Gold, frankincense, and myrrh present.

4. Laud to the Holy Trinity,
   All thanks and praise to God most high.

Quem Pastores Laudavere
WHOM OF OLD THE SHEPHERDS PRAISED

Hohenfurth Manuscript
Translation: G.R. Woodward, 1902
(Altered: GKE)

Hohenfurth Manuscript, 1410

Andante

1. Quem pas-to-res lau-da-ver-e, Qui-bus an-ge-li-dix-e-re, Ab-sit vo-bis jam ti-me-re, Na-tus est Rex glo-ri-ae.

1. Whom of old the shep-herds prais-ed, When the ser-aph them up-rais-ed, Say-ing, "Sirs, be not a-maz-ed, Heav'n's all-glo-rious King is born!"

2. *Ad quem magi ambulabant,*
   Aurum, thus, myrrham portabant,
   Immolabant haec sincere
   Leoni victoriae.

2. Unto whom the kings came faring
   Gold and myrrh and incense bearing,
   Love unfeignedly declaring
   For the conqu'ring Child of God.

317

Adeste Fideles

O COME, ALL YE FAITHFUL

J.F. Wade
Translation: Frederick Oakley, alt. 1841

J.F. Wade, ca 1740

ni - te a - do - re - mus___ Do - mi - num.
come, let us a - dore___ Him,___ Christ,___ the Lord.

2. *Cantet nunc Io! chorus angelorum;*
   Cantet nunc aula caelestium:
   Gloria, gloria, in excelsis Deo:
   Venite adoremus, etc.

2. Sing, choirs of angels, sing in exultation,
   Sing, all ye citizens of heav'n above!
   Glory to God, all glory in the highest!
   O come, let us adore Him, etc.

3. *Ergo qui natus die hodierna,*
   Jesu, tibi sit gloria!
   Patris aeterni Verbum caro factum:
   Venite adoremus, etc.

3. Yea, Lord, we greet Thee, born this holy
      morning,
   Jesus, to Thee be glory giv'n!
   Word of the Father, now in flesh
      appearing:
   O come, let us adore Him, etc.

ADESTE FIDELES, page 318. Only recently have the true historical facts about this hymn become known, and we have Dom John Stéphan of Buckfast Abbey to thank for them. By diligent research in old manuscripts he discovered that both the Latin words and the music were written by J. F. Wade (1711–1786), an Englishman who spent his life copying and teaching music at the Roman Catholic center in Douay, France. He composed *Adeste Fideles* between 1740 and 1745.

The English translation was made by Reverend Francis Oakeley in 1841, while he was Rector of All Saints' Anglican Church in London. A few years later, Oakeley joined the Roman Catholic church and eventually became a Bishop. The opening lines of his translation read:

> Ye faithful, approach ye,
> Joyfully triumphant.

The familiar words, *O Come, All Ye Faithful,* first appeared in a revision printed in 1852.

ALL MY HEART THIS NIGHT REJOICES, page 59. Although its text was originally German, we have classified this as an American carol because the tune is by a prominent American composer of the nineteenth century, Horatio Parker (1863–1919). A leading organist and for many years head of the music department at Yale, Dr. Parker also composed hymns; an opera, *Mona,* produced by the Metropolitan Opera in 1911; and an oratorio, *Hora Novissima,* that is still considered to be one of the finest examples of the form in the romantic style.

Paul Gerhardt (1607–1676), author of the text, was one of the greatest German hymn writers, ranking with Martin Luther. He was a successful minister in the Lutheran church, but was forbidden to preach for a time for refusing to subscribe to some tenets of the Cal-

vanists. Catherine Winkworth, who made the translation of Gerhardt's poem used here, wrote of him: "His preaching is said to have been very earnest and persuasive, and full of Christian love and charity, which he practised as well as preached by never turning a beggar from his doors, and receiving widows and orphans who needed help and shelter into his own house."

The hymn's German title is *Fröhlich Soll Mein Herze Springen.* Two of its verses (Numbers 1 and 3 of the Winkworth translation) are:

> *Fröhlich soll mein Herze springen*
> *Dieser Zeit, da vor Freud*
> *Alle Engel singen!*
> *Hört, hört wie mit vollen Chören,*
> *Alle Luft laute ruft:*
> *Christus ist geboren.*
>
> *Ei, so kommt und lasst uns laufen,*
> *Stellt euch ein, gross und klein,*
> *Kommt mit grossen Haufen.*
> *Liebt den, der vor Liebe brennet,*
> *Schaut den Stern, der euch gern,*
> *Liebt un Labsal gönnet.*

ALS ICH BEI MEINEN SCHAFEN WACHT, page 146, is from a sixteenth century nativity play. A shepherd sang the solo verses onstage, and was answered in the echoes by an offstage angelic chorus.

ANGELS FROM THE REALMS OF GLORY, page 49. Henry Smart (1813–1869) was a well-known London organist and composer. He was particularly noted for his improviations at the organ.

James Montgomery (1771–1814), a Scotchman, was the editor of the Sheffield *Iris,* a newspaper. He was also the writer of many devout hymns. The text of *Angels from the Realms of Glory* first appeared in the *Iris* of December 24, 1816.

AS WITH GLADNESS MEN OF OLD, page 48. Conrad Kocher was editor of a collection of German chorales published in 1838 under the title *Stimmen aus dem Reiches Gottes* (Voices from the Kingdom of God). One of the selections included, *"Treuer Heiland, wir sind hier! (Faithful Savior, We Come to Thee),"* was later abridged to provide the music for this Christmas hymn. The same tune is used in *For the Beauty of the Earth*, widely sung at Thanksgiving services.

William Dix, author of the text, is mentioned in the notes on the carol, *What Child Is This?*

AWAY IN A MANGER, page 60, was for many years attributed to Martin Luther. Investigations by Richard Hill in the 1940s proved conclusively that Luther had nothing to do with the carol. J. R. Murray, the American harmonizer of the melody, seems to have been chiefly responsible for the misrepresentation. He labeled his setting "Luther's Cradle Hymn," and added the note: "composed by Martin Luther for his children, and still sung by German mothers everywhere." The source of the tune is still unknown, but it was likely composed by a member of the German Lutheran colony of Pennsylvania. The anonymous words for the first two stanzas appeared in the *Little Children's Book for Schools and Families*, published in 1885 by the Evangelical Lutheran Church in North America. A third stanza was added later, and even its authorship is uncertain.

BALLADE DE JÉSUS-CHRIST, page 114, is one treatment of a wide-spread, middle-European legend that tells of the return of Christ to earth during the Christmas season as a ragged, hungry child. When given food and shelter, the child reveals his true identity and gives a blessing to his benefactor. French versions of the legend are almost always titled Ballads of Jesus Christ. This particular carol probably dates from the seventeenth century.

BARN JESUS, page 190, is a collaboration by two of Denmark's most illustrious artists: Hans Christian Andersen, the teller of tales, and Niels Gade, often referred to as the Father of Danish Music.

BEHOLD THAT STAR, page 78. Both words and music of this spiritual are by Thomas W. Talley. At the time he wrote it, Mr. Talley was a faculty member of Fisk University in Nashville, Tennessee, and was director of the Mozart Society (later known as the Fisk University Choir). Mr. Talley was looking for a Christmas number that would capture the spirit of a jubilee song. He wrote, "As the son of an ex-slave, I knew a great many jubilee songs, but none pertained to Christmas." After a fruitless search, Talley decided he would have to compose an original jubilee carol. *Behold That Star* was the result. In teaching the song to the choir, Talley refrained from letting them know it was his own com-

position. They assumed they were singing a traditional jubilee song. It was only some time later, when Talley's daughter, who was studying at the Juilliard School of Music, made arrangements to have the carol published in a folk song collection that he revealed that he was its creator.

John Work, the present director of the Fisk University Choir, remembers Mr. Talley well, and corroborates his story of how *Behold That Star* came into being.

BERGER, SECOUE TON SOMMEIL PROFOUND, page 122. A Besançon carol that appeared in the *Recueil de Noëls anciens au patois de Besançon*, published in 1842. The tune presumably dates from the seventeenth century.

BLESSED BE THAT MAID MARIE, page 41, appeared in William Ballet's Lute Book, issued in manuscript in 1594. The madrigal-like style of the carol reflects the refining influences of composers such as Palestrina, Lassus, and Byrd which were bringing about a departure from the rustic simplicity of folk carols.

THE BOAR'S HEAD CAROL, page 34, has been used in the Christmas festivities at Queen's College, Oxford, for over 500 years. According to legend, a student at the college was walking through some nearby woods on Christmas day when a wild boar attacked him. The scholar was browsing in a book by Aristotle at the time, and since the book was his only available defense, he shoved it down the boar's throat. The animal immediately rolled over and died. The student severed the boar's head and carried it back to the college. That evening, it was served to the student body with great ceremony. True or not, this story is the basis of the Queen's College custom of ushering in the boar's head with the singing of this carol during the Christmas dinner. One of the earliest carols to appear in print, Wynken de Worde included *The Boar's Head* in his collection, *Christmasse Carolles*, published in 1521.

Other boar's head carols have come down to us from the Middle Ages. Several are printed in Greene's collection of manuscript carols, indicating that serving of the delicacy on Christmas Day was a widespread practice.

BRICH AN, DU SCHÖNES MORGENLICHT, page 162, is taken from Bach's *Christmas Oratorio*. In Part II, it follows the appearance of the angels to the shepherds. The text by Johann Rist and the chorale setting by Johann Schop first appeared in *Himmlische Lieder* (1641). Bach altered Schop's music extensively in his harmonization.

BRIGHTEST AND BEST (STAR OF THE EAST), page 88. This folk setting of Bishop Heber's famous hymn on the Epiphany has a magnificent solemnity about it that imbues the text with an impressive feeling of awe.

CANTIQUE DE NOËL, page 107. Adolphe Adam (1803–1856) gained fame for a time as a composer of ballets. Today, he is chiefly remembered for one ballet, *Giselle*, and this carol.

The English translation is by John S. Dwight (1813–1893), co-founder of the Harvard Music Society.

CANZONE D'I ZAMPOGNARI, page 242. For centuries, the peasants from the Abruzzi mountains have strolled the streets of Naples during the nine days before Christmas, playing and singing carols before an image of the Baby Jesus. They usually travel in pairs, one playing the bagpipe and the other a clarinet-like instrument, the *ciaramella*. It is thought that Handel heard this carol during his Italian travels and later adapted its melody for "He Shall Feed His Flock" in *Messiah*.

CÉLÉBRONS LA NAISSANCE, page 92. The melody has been known throughout France since the fifteenth century and has been sung to numerous sacred and secular texts. Lucas le Moigne's words, *Or, nous dites Marie*, were written before 1450. The verses used here were included in *La Grande Bible des Noëls*, dated 1766.

CHIQUIRRIQUITIN, page 280. Many Spanish carols are known as *villancicos*, a poetic form with a history reaching back to the fourteenth century. A refrain begins and ends the songs, with verses sung in between. Each province has developed its own melody and words for the *villancicos*, and they are usually sung in the local dialect. The favorite subject for the text is the visit of the shepherds to the manger, but lullabys are also very popular.

CHTIC, ABY SPAL, page 234. The poverty and humility of the first Christmas are often stressed in Polish and Czechoslovakian carols, but they are pictured as natural, admirable, and often joyful conditions. This reflects the predominantly peasant origin of both their texts and music, as do the subjects they treat: almost all are pastoral songs or lullabys.

COVENTRY CAROL, page 19, was included in the *Pageant of the Shearmen and Tailors' Guilds*, a mystery play performed in Coventry, England, as early as the fifteenth century. Many members of the English royal family witnessed the presentation, among them King Richard III. In the play, the carol is sung by the women of Bethlehem just before their children are killed by Herod's soldiers.

DECK THE HALL WITH BOUGHS OF HOLLY, page 53. Very little is known about this lively Welsh carol, but it is quite old. Mozart used its melody in a violin and piano duet composed around 1700.

DE TIERRA LEJANA VENIMOS, page 288. The Feast of the Epiphany is the most important holiday of the Christmas season in Puerto Rico. The children set out containers of food and drink for the Three Wise Men and their camels on that day, because it is the Magi that bring them presents. This custom originated in Spain, and is still observed in almost all Spanish-speaking lands.

DORS, MA COLOMBE, page 120. The province of Alsace lies between France and Germany, and the languages of both countries are spoken there. The translation given with this carol is of the French words, but the German text that follows, dating from 1697, is sung by many Alsatians:

1. *Schlaf', mein Kindelein, schlaf', mein Söhnelein,*
   Singt die Mutter Jungfrau rein.
   Schlaf', mein Herzelein, schlaf', mein Schätzelein,
   Singt der Vater eben fein.
   Refrain:
   Singet und klinget dem Kindelein klein,
   Dem hönigsüssen Jesulein!
   Singet und klinget, ihr Engelein rein
   Mit tausend süssen Stimmelein.

2. *Schliess' die Augelein, deck' dein' Händelein,*
   Denn es braust ein scharfer Wind;
   Schlaf', mein Kindelein, dich das Eselein
   Wird erwärmen mit dem Rind.
   Refrain

3. *Schlaf', mein Hoffnung und mein Tröstung,*
   Schlaf', O Freund des Herzens mein!
   Schlaf', mein Wonne, schlaf', mein Krone,
   Schlaf' und schliess dein' Augelein!
   Refrain

EL RORRO, page 308. On Christmas Eve as the climax of the *Posada* ceremonies, an image of the Baby Jesus is placed in a manger and carolers gather around to sing this lullaby.

EN BELEN TOCAN A FUEGO, page 276. Although every country has carols reporting miraculous events occurring when Christ was born, Spain offers a particularly rich variety of them. This carol appears to be the only example in which even the fish of the river rejoice over Jesus' birth.

EN NOMBRE DEL CIELO, page 306. The *Posada* is performed in Mexico for nine nights preceding Christmas. The word means "lodging," and the ceremony re-enacts the search for shelter in Bethlehem the night of Jesus' birth. A procession carrying candles and images of Mary and Joseph stops at a chosen house, and the leader knocks at the door. When the door is opened, this carol is sung as a dialogue between the owner of the house and the visitor pleading for shelter. At the conclusion of the song, all the members of the group are invited into

322

the house for refreshments, dancing, and the breaking of the *Piñata*.

A container made of earthenware or *papier-mâché*, the *Piñata* is stuffed with candies, fruit, and good luck charms. It is hung from the ceiling and blindfolded guests lash out at it with wooden paddles. When a paddle makes contact, the *Piñata* shatters, and its contents fly in all directions. Everyone scrambles to pick up the largest share of the favors.

ES IST EIN' ROS' ENTSPRUNGEN, page 166. Both words and music were printed in the *Speierschen Gesangbuch* published in Cologne in 1600. The beautiful harmonization, which appeared in *Musae Sioniae* (1609), is by Michael Praetorius, a famous musical theorist and composer. The German words are a paraphrase of the eleventh chapter of Isaiah, verse 1: "And there shall come forth a rod out of the stem of Jesse, and a branch shall grow out of his roots." Dr. Theodore Baker (1851–1934), eminent musicologist and author of *Baker's Biographical Dictionary of Music and Musicians,* made the English translation.

ES WIRD SCHO GLEI DUMPA, page 172. Lullaby carols such as this are sung around the *krippe* in Austrian homes.

ET BARN ER FØDT I BETHLEHEM, page 192 is a setting derived from the famous Latin hymn, *Puer Natus in Bethlehem,* which appears on page 316.

THE FIRST NOWELL, page 26, one of the oldest Ballad Carols, has stayed in the front rank of popularity through the centuries. Sandys (1833) gives the earliest known printed version, but the carol is at least 250 or 300 years older. In spite of having its name misspelled "Noel" occasionally, it has never had any French associations. As English as plum pudding, it probably originated in Cornwall.

THE FRIENDLY BEASTS, page 24. The tune used here is the Latin hymn, *Orientis Partibus,* which accompanied the Donkey's Festival of the twelfth century (see page 6). The modern words were written by Robert Davis in 1949. Because of its simple melody and fanciful text, the carol has great appeal for children.

GLOUCESTERSHIRE WASSAIL, page 32. A special custom was observed in connection with this carol in Gloucestershire about 160 years ago. A band of carolers paraded through the streets carrying a huge bowl decorated with ribbons and filled with spiced ale. As the musicians sang, they freely dispensed the wassail, so it was literally "Wassail, wassail, all over the town!"

GOD REST YOU MERRY, GENTLEMEN, page 18. The music uses the natural minor scale, a very unusual choice for a cheerful song, but it works beautifully here. Sandys included the text in his 1833 collection. The melody is probably much older than the words.

In *A Christmas Carol,* Dickens tells how Scrooge was busy in his counting house on Christmas Eve when a half-starved youth stopped by to regale him with a Christmas carol. Dickens wrote: "At the first sound of 'God rest you merry, gentlemen, Let nothing you dismay!', Scrooge seized the ruler with such energy of action that the singer fled in terror."

GOOD CHRISTIAN MEN, REJOICE, page 12. An English version of one of Germany's most beloved carols, both the tune and words have a complicated and interesting history. The music originally appeared in the famous Finnish carol collection, *Piae Cantiones* (1582). Germany adopted the tune in the fourteenth century, adding macaronic words. (Macaronic texts combine lines in Latin with a vernacular language. The practice appears in medieval manuscript carols and probably rose from the efforts of priests to inject some spiritual content into folk carols).

The German setting, with an English translation by R. L. de Pearsall (1795–1856), is:

Legend has it that Henry Suso (died 1366), a German Dominican, was visited by angels who invited him to dance and sing this song with them. When he awoke, he wrote down the Latin-German words and tune.

Dr. Neale has made a free paraphrase of the original German text in *Good Christian Men, Rejoice,* but has retained its spirit. Helmore transcribed his music directly from *Piae Cantiones,* but in the process, he made an error in interpreting the original notation. He assigned a value equivalent to two dotted *half* notes (on the words, "News! News!" in the first verse) where the value should have been equivalent to two *eighth* notes. Today, we find the resulting rhythmic eccentricity charming!

GOOD KING WENCESLAS, page 17. As with many other fine carols, we have the *Piae Cantiones* to thank for the tune used here by Helmore. It was originally a spring carol, *Tempus adest floridum*. Helmore adhered to the original melody, but Dr. Neale composed an entirely new text. He has been widely criticized for the result by many carol authorities who have called his verses everything from "doggerel" to "poor and commonplace to the last degree." All Neale wanted to do was to write a carol for Saint Stephen's Day (December 26), basing it on an old Bohemian legend about Saint Wenceslaus. Authorities or no authorities, the carol continues to be a great favorite. It is one of few modern carols that departs from the Scriptures and tells a miraculous story in the medieval style.

HARK, THE HERALD ANGELS SING, page 46, was intended by its author, Charles Wesley, to be a hymn dealing with the Incarnation rather than Christmas. His original opening lines were:

> Hark, how all the welkin rings,
> Glory to the King of kings.

George Whitfield, Charles' personal friend and associate in the development of Methodism, altered the lines to include the herald angels.

Wesley's stanzas were four lines long, and were probably originally sung to a simple hymn tune. Over a hundred years after the text was written, William Cummings, organist of Waltham Abbey, rearranged the words into ten-line stanzas and set them to a chorus from Mendelssohn's cantata written to celebrate the invention of printing, the *Festgesang*.

THE HOLLY AND THE IVY, page 22. During the Middle Ages, these two plants came to be associated with the sexes, holly being masculine and ivy feminine. Many jokes grew up about the two in which they were protagonists in domestic squabbles as to whom had authority around the house. This fifteenth century carol offers an example in the vein:

> Holly and Ivy made a great party,
> Who should have the mastery
> In landes where they go.

> Then spake Holly, "I am free and jolly,
> I will have the mastery,
> In landes where we go."

> Then spake Ivy, "I am loved and proud,
> And I will have the mastery,
> In landes where we go."

> Then spake Holly, and set him on his knee,
> "I pray thee, gentle Ivy,
> Say me no villainy
> In landes where we go."

In *The Holly and the Ivy*, secular and comical elements are missing; its spirit, while cheerful, is much more devotional. Erik Routley says its purpose is to recite the acts of Redemption symbolized by the blossom, berry, thorns and bark of the holly tree.

HUSH, MY BABE, LIE STILL AND SLUMBER, page 87, was the closing song in Isaac Watts' collection, *Divine and Moral Songs for Children*, published in 1715. The highly moralistic texts exhort children to rise early, to avoid roughness in play, to be industrious, not to steal, and generally, to be perfect little ladies and gentlemen. The Kentucky mountain tune with its parallel harmonies and modal touches lends a special charm to the carol.

ICH STEH' AN DEINER KRIPPE HIER, page 163. Bach used this chorale in the final section of the *Christmas Oratorio*. It is sung by the congregation immediately after the Magi have presented their gifts to the Babe.

Paul Gehrhardt has been mentioned in the notes for *All My Heart This Night Rejoices*.

I HEARD THE BELLS ON CHRISTMAS DAY, page 58. In 1863, Henry W. Longfellow's son, a lieutenant in the Army of the Potomac, was seriously wounded in battle. This event inspired the father to write this rather melancholy but hopeful poem. Longfellow had no intention for it to be used as a carol. The tune by J. Baptiste Calkin (1829-1905) was composed for an entirely different purpose than to go with Longfellow's words. We do not know who joined the words and music. In spite of all this fortuitouness, the carol has great significance in today's troubled world.

IHR KINDERLEIN, KOMMET, page 142. At the age of 15, Johann Abraham Peter Schultz, the composer of this carol, journeyed to Berlin to study organ with J. S. Bach's pupil, Kirnberger. Schultz mastered the organ in an amazingly short time, and his virtuoso playing attracted the attention of the royalty of the entire continent, bringing him invitations to play at courts in France, Italy and Germany. After touring extensively, he settled in Denmark, where he served as the King's *Kapellmeister* for eight years.

As a writer of songs, Schultz was very particular about the texts he chose, insisting that they be works of art in their own right. Christoph von Schmid's verses for this carol have proved to be a happy choice, for it has been one of the most endearing and enduring children's Christmas songs for almost 200 years.

IL EST NÉ, LE DIVIN ENFANT, page 94, is set to the melody of an eighteenth century Air de Chasse, *La Tête Bizarde*.

I SAW THREE SHIPS, page 52. A legend with a long history lies behind this carol. It begins with the Magi. After their deaths, the remains of the Three Wise Men were reportedly transferred to Byzantium by the Empress Helena, mother of Emperor Constantine. Later, they were transferred to Milan. And still later, in 1162, three ships carried their skulls to Cologne at the command of Frederick Barbarossa. With time, the three skulls were transmuted into the persons of Christ and his mother, and *I Saw Three Ships* had them sailing into Bethlehem on Christmas morning.

IT CAME UPON THE MIDNIGHT CLEAR, page 62, has a text written by Edmund H. Sears, a Harvard-trained Unitarian clergyman. The poem was first publishing in the *Christian Register* in 1850. The editor of that journal, also a clergyman, some years later said of this carol: "I always feel that, however, poor my Christmas sermon may be, the reading and singing of this hymn are enough to make up for all deficiencies."

Richard S. Willis had another hymn, *See Israel's Gentle Shepherd Stand*, in mind when he wrote the music associated with this carol, but its pairing with these words formed a close union. Willis, whose father was founder of *The Youth's Companion* magazine, graduated from Yale and later studied music in Europe. One of his teachers was Felix Mendelssohn.

JEG ER SAA GLAD HVER JULEKVELD, page 202. The Norwegians emphasize the serious and religious side of Christmas, but the children have ample opportunity for fun-making. A prankish elf named *Jule-nissen*, who hides in the attic or barn during the year, comes out at midnight on Christmas Eve to distribute presents. He has long, white whiskers and wears a pointed cap. His habit is to ride into the middle of Christmas Eve celebrations mounted on a goat. He loves to chase the children, making them scamper to get out of his way. After making several turns about the room handing out gifts, *Jule-nissen* is out the door and gone until next Christmas.

JOSEF, LIEBER JOSEF MEIN, page 148. was sung around the crib of the Christ Child in a mystery play dating from the late fifteenth century. The melody bears the Latin name *Resonet in Laudibus*.

JOY TO THE WORLD, page 28. The melody has been credited to various composers, among them Handel and Lowell Mason, but its origin has never been determined.

The text is from Isaac Watts' *Psalms of David Imitated in the Language of the New Testament*, published in 1719. It is an adaptation of Psalm 98, which includes the lines, "Make a joyful noise unto the Lord, all the earth."

KLING, GLÖCKCHEN, page 140. Still another recounting of Christ's return to earth at Christmas, this time accompanied by his mother.

LA MARCHE DES ROIS, page 126. Both the words and melody of this Noël from Provence are extremely old, having been sung as early as the thirteenth century.

Since the action of Alphonse Daudet's tragedy, *L'Arlesienne*, takes place on Christmas Eve, Georges Bizet used an arrangement of *La Marche des Rois* to create a Christmas atmosphere in his incidental music to the play.

LES ANGES DANS NOS CAMPAGNES, page 96. In England, James Montgomery's hymn, *Angels from the Realms of Glory*, is the favored text for this melody. The origin of the carol is uncertain; it probably dates from the eighteenth century.

LE SOMMEIL DE L'ENFANT JÉSUS, page 100. Francois Gevaert (1828–1905), director of the Brussels Conservatory for many years, is often credited with writing this carol. He made the best-known harmonization of it, but the melody is an Angevin folk song that is probably 200 years old.

LIPPAI, page 168, is very popular in the Austrian Tirol and the Salzburg vicinity, the same locale that gave us *Silent Night*. The tune is very much like typical Austrian country dances called *Ländler*.

LULAJZE JEZUNIU, page 220. Chopin used the melody of this beautiful lullaby carol in his *Scherzo in B Minor, Opus 20*.

MARIA DURCH EIN' DORNWALD GING, page 160, exhibits characteristics of the earliest German religious folk songs that indicate it dates from the fifteenth century. Among these are a missing seventh degree of the scale in the melody, and the use of the macaronic text.

MASTERS IN THIS HALL, page 50. The organist of Chartres Cathedral gave this old French tune to Edmund Sedding, an English compiler of Christmas carols. Sedding asked William Morris (1834–1896), who worked in the same office with him, to write some verses to fit the tune. Morris, an extraordinarily gifted and versatile man, was a painter and inventor (of the Morris chair, for one example) as well as a poet. In this text, and in others he wrote, Morris remarkably recaptures the vigor and flavor of the old medieval carols. Sedding included the Chartres tune with Morris' words in his *Antient Christmas Carols,* published in 1860.

NAR JULDAGSMORGON GLIMMAR, page 194. In Sweden, the Christmas season begins on Santa Lucia Day, December 13. Early on that morning, one of the women or girls of the household dons a long white dress with a red sash, places a crown of lighted candles on her head, and carries hot coffee to the other members of the family, singing carols as she serves them. The veneration of an Italian saint by the Swedish people has been a tradition ever since the Vikings were converted to Christianity.

NESEM VAM NOVINY, page 236. Bohemia lies between Germany and Czechoslovakia, and is bi-lingual. Our music is given with the Czech text and its translation. The following German words, written by Karl Riedel (1827–1888) are also widely sung:

> *Kommet, ihr Hirten, ihr Männer und Fraun.*
> *Kommet, das liebliche Kindlein zuschaun.*
> *Christus, der Herr, is heute geboren,*
> *Dem Gott zum Heiland euch erkoren.*
> *Fürchtet euch nicht!*
>
> *Lasset uns sehen in Bethlehems Stall,*
> *Was uns verheissen der himmlische Schall!*
> *Was wir dort finden, lasset uns künden,*
> *Lasset uns preisen in frommen Weisen!*
> *Halleluja!*
>
> *Wahrlich, die Engel verkündigen heut*
> *Bethlehems Hirtenvolk gar grosse Freud.*
> *Nun soll es werden Friede auf Erden,*
> *Den Menschen allen ein Wohlgefallen.*
> *Ehre sei Gott!*

The melody of this carol, a Bohemian folk song, dates from 1870.

NOEL DES AUSELS, page 124. William J. Phillips, in his book, *Carols, Their Origin and History,* comments that God made the world a garden at the time of its creation, and that it was only Adam's sin that deprived mankind of its delights. Nature's beauty was still with us, however, and Phillips observed: "It is only natural that poets should associate the beauty, purity, and innocence of God's creation with the perfection of the Christ-Child, born to redeem the world." Accordingly, many carols link Man and Nature together in the blessings of the Incarnation. Phillips specifically mentions this old carol from Bas-Quercy (now Basses-Pyrénées), near the Spanish border in Southwestern France, in which different birds sing their homage to Jesus. The melody of the carol is probably over 400 years old.

NÖEL NOUVELET, page 118. Marcel Dupre's well-known organ composition, *Variations on a French Noël,* is based on this melody, which is in the Dorian mode.

NU AR DET JUL IGEN, page 193. This lively carol is written to the rhythm of Sweden's most popular folk dance, the *Hambo.* A favorite holiday pastime for Swedish children is to form a circle around the Christmas tree and sing and dance *Nu Är Det Jul Igen.*

O DU FRÖHLICHE, page 136. Originally a hymn of praise to the Virgin Mary, O *Sanctissima,* the text has undergone many translations and changes; in several instances, it has emerged with Christmas words.

The tune is known as the Sicilian Mariner's Hymn, but no one has been able to trace its origin to either Sicily or sailors. It seems to have been composed in the latter part of the eighteenth century and may have been an aria from an opera of the period.

O LITTLE TOWN OF BETHLEHEM, page 63. Phillips Brooks was one of the truly great preachers America has produced. In December 1865, he visited the Holy Land, and on the day before Christmas, he rode horseback from Jerusalem to Bethlehem. The journey ended with Brooks coming upon Bethlehem resting peacefully under the night sky of winter. Three years later, back in Philadelphia and wanting to write a Christmas carol for the children of his congregation, he recalled his first glimpse of the village and wrote the words to *O Little Town of Bethlehem.* He asked his church organist and Sunday School superintendent, Lewis H. Redner, to write some music for his poem. All during Christmas week, Redner struggled to write an appropriate tune, but he had not thought of one that satisfied him when he retired to his bed on Christmas Eve. During the night, he woke with "an angel strain" sounding in his ears. He jotted the melody down immediately and wrote the harmony for it early the next morning. He always referred to the tune as his "gift from heaven."

Trying to determine a name for their carol, Redner urged that it be called *Saint Phillips.* "No," said Brooks, "we will call it *Saint Louis.*" The hymn tune has had this name ever since.

ONCE IN ROYAL DAVID'S CITY, page 44, was one of Mrs. Cecil Frances Alexander's *Hymns for Little Children* (1848), designed to explain the Catechism. *There Is a Green Hill Far Away* was another poem in the same series. Mrs. Alexander was the wife of the Primate of all Ireland.

The words of the carol were linked almost immediately with Gauntlett's tune, *Irby,* and the two have remained partners ever since. Dr. Gauntlett was an organist and organ designer as well as a composer. Mendelssohn once said of him:

His literary attainments, his knowledge of the history of music, his acquaintance with acoustical laws, his marvelous memory, his philosophical turn of mind, as well as his practical experience, rendered him one of the most remarkable professors of his age.

O TANNENBAUM, 138. We have no reliable information concerning the origin of the Christmas tree. One story told throughout Germany is an expansion of the legend of Christ's return to earth as a starving child (see notes on the *Ballade de Jésus-Christ*). In this version, after the child was brought into the house, warmed, and fed, a radiance filled the room and the Angelic Host again appeared to sing *Glorias*. As he left the cottage, the Christ Child broke a branch from a fir tree and pushed it into the earth. Immediately, it burst into bloom. "This is my gift to you," Jesus said. "Each Christmas henceforth, it shall bloom again, reaffirming my love for mankind."

Most evidence indicates the Christmas tree is a descendent of the pagan reverence for evergreen boughs and their magic power to ward off evil. This was probably one of the reasons that the Church has strongly disapproved of the use of evergreen trees in Christmas observances from time to time. It had other objections. In 1740, Konrad Dannhauer of Strassburg complained:

> Among other trifles with which people often occupy the Christmas time is the Christmas tree, which they erect in the house, hang with dolls and sugar and cause to lose its bloom. Where the habit comes from, I do not know. Far better that children be dedicated to the spiritual cedar tree, Jesus Christ.

A 1561 Alsatian ordinance seems to be the earliest extant mention of the use of evergreen trees for Christmas decoration. It forbade the cutting of bushes "more than the length of eight shoes" for Christmas adornments.

In the beginning, the trees were hung upside down from the rafters and decorated with fruits, gilded nuts, and colored ribbons of paper. By the middle of the sixteenth century, they had assumed an upright position, and candles and tinsel became part of the ornamentation.

From Alsace, the lighted Christmas tree traveled to all parts of German-speaking Europe, to England, to Scandinavia, and eventually, to America. One report states that the Hessian soldiers brought the tree to the United States during the Revolutionary War. Prince Albert is said to have introduced it to Victorian England. Beyond English and Germanic lands, the tree has received only limited acceptance. Most other countries cling to the *crèche* as their chief Christmas symbol.

PAT-A-PAN, page 112. The words, given in their original Burgundian dialect, appeared in *Noëls Bourgignons de Bernard de la Monnoye*, 1842. Bernard de la Monnoye (1641–1728) wrote many lively songs and carols, including some notably ribald ones.

PUER NATUS IN BETHLEHEM, page 316. During the fourteenth century, new words, called a *trope*, were added to the Christmas service. The trope was inserted into the priest's chant near the end of the service between the words *Benedicamus Domino* and the response, *Deo Gratias*. The melody of this carol developed as a counter-melody to the trope, eventually supplanting the original tune.

QUEM PASTORES LAUDAVERE, page 317. Members of early German choirs copied the music of hymns they sang by hand into special books. Because this carol was a great favorite, it was usually the first number copied. As a result, the collections came to be known as *Quempass* books, a name coined from a contraction of the first two words of this song.

QUITTEZ, PASTEURS, page 98, is from the province of Anjou. The words were included in Garnier's *La Grande Bible Renouvelée de Noëls Nouveau*, published in 1728. The melody is from one of the most popular songs of its day (around 1875), *Nanon Dormait*.

QUOI, MA VOISINE, ES-TU FÂCHÉE? page 104, has a text that first appeared in print around 1875. The tune is much older. The dialogue between two women that ends with a joint prayer for humility has a rustic gossip touch that we have tried to preserve in the translation.

RISE UP, SHEPHERD, AND FOLLOW, page 80. Practically nothing is known of the source of this spiritual, or of the several that follow it in our collection. The simple, frequently poignant lyrics and the rhythmic, tuneful music of spirituals give a unique dimension to the celebration of Christmas.

SEL BYCH RÁD K BETLÉMU, page 232. The melody was originally a hymn tune, as was that of the carol that follows, CHTIC, ABY SPAL, TAK ZPÍVALA, page 234. Simon, in his *Treasury of Christmas Songs and Carols*, says such carols were probably written by village priests, who were also the schoolmasters, for their students.

THE SEVEN JOYS OF MARY, page 14, is one of many numeral carols. This particular example first existed as a medieval manuscript carol, wherein the joys were limited to five. That version enjoyed great popularity during the fifteenth century in England. Some eighteenth and nineteenth century treatments increased the joys to twelve. The seven-verse form given here has become the standard one. The mention of the Crucifixion in stanza six reflects the practice of including references to the Passion during the Christmas season that appeared during the era of the Ballad Carols.

SLEEP, HOLY BABE, page 45. The words are by Reverend Edward Caswell, a Church of England clergyman who later became a Roman Catholic. Caswell was noted for his skillful translations of Latin hymns into English, many of which still appear in present-day hymnals.

Dr. Dykes, the composer, was also an ordained clergyman of the Anglican church. He served as Precentor (Choirmaster) of Durham Cathedral for a number of years.

SLICZNA PANIENKA, page 216. Straw, representing the manger and stable of Bethlehem, is a revered Christmas symbol in many Eastern European countries. It is placed under the tablecloth at Christmas meals and strewn under rugs upon which the family kneels for Christmas prayers.

STILLE NACHT, HEILIGE NACHT, page 176. On Christmas Eve, 1818, the organ in Saint Nicholas Church in Oberndorf, Austria, broke down. This left the organist, Franz Gruber, in a critical position, for all the numbers planned for that evening's service relied on an organ accompaniment. This statement by Gruber explained what followed:

> Josef Mohr, then assistant pastor of the newly established...church, handed to Franz Gruber, who was attending to the duties of organist (and was at the same time a schoolmaster in Arnsdorf) a poem, with the request that he write for it a suitable melody arranged for two solo voices, chorus, and guitar accompaniment. On that very same evening the latter, in fulfillment of this request made to him as a music expert, handed to the pastor his simple composition, which was thereupon immediately performed on that holy night of Christmas Eve and received with all acclaim.

Shortly after Christmas, an organ tuner from the *Zillerthal* came to repair the instrument, and Gruber played the new carol for him. The repairman was so pleased with it that he carried a copy away with him and showed it to the Strasser Sisters, a famous troupe of Tyrolean singers. They added *Silent Night* to their repertoire, and everywhere they went on their extensive tours it was the favorite selection. Its popularity spread far and wide, but the names of Mohr and Gruber were never mentioned as its creators. Franz Joseph Haydn's son, Michael, was given credit for the carol in some published copies, possibly because he may have made an arrangement of the music. In 1854, 47 years after its composition, a special government committee was set up to try to determine who the creators of *Silent Night* were. They unearthed the true facts through Felix Gruber, the son of Franz, who submitted the above statement by his father to them, along with a copy of the original carol.

SUSANI, page 152, is one of the oldest German carols. Early versions date back to the fourteenth century.

THERE'S A SONG IN THE AIR, page 61. Josiah G. Holland (1819–1881), the author of this poem, studied medicine for a time, but eventually changed to preparation for a literary career. After serving for some years as a newspaper editor and writing several books, he formed a partnership with Roswell Smith and founded *Scribner's Magazine* in 1869. For the rest of his life, Holland was editor of *Scribner's*.

Karl Harrington (1861–1953) was a college professor whose major teaching field was classical languages. He wrote the musical setting used for this carol while on a summer vacation in the mountains of his native New Hampshire. It was published in 1920. Harrington's ability as a composer was so highly regarded that Wesleyan University conferred an honorary Doctor of Music degree upon him in 1946.

THIS ENDRIS NIGHT, page 16, is a lullaby carol. The title means "the other night," or "several nights ago." The words stem from manuscript carols of the late Middle Ages, but take on the characteristics of the Ballad Carols. They were first written down the latter part of the fifteenth century. The tune, definitely a Ballad Carol, was recorded about a century later, around 1600.

THE WINTER MOON SHONE COLD AND CLEAR, page 76, is set to an old French folk tune. The words were written in the Huron Indian language by Father Jean de Brebeuf, a Jesuit missionary to the Iroquois and Huron tribes of Canada. In 1642, Father Brebeuf wrote this comment on the attitude of the Indians toward Christmas:

> The savages have a particular devotion for the night that was enlightened by the birth of the Son of God. There was not one who refused to fast on the day that preceded it. They built a small chapel of cedar and fir branches in honor of the manger of the infant Jesus. They wished to perform some penance to prepare themselves for better receiving Him into their hearts on that holy day, and even those who were at a distance of more than two day's journey met at a given place to sing hymns in honor of the new-born child.

Father Brebeuf's original words to the carol make a wonderful music on their own, even without benefit of a melody or harmonic accompaniment, as can be seen from this first verse:

> *Estennialon de tsonue Iesus ahatonnia,*
> *Onnauateua 'd'oki n'onandaskuaentak;*
> *Enonchien skuatrihotat n'onuandilonrachatha,*
> *Iesua ahatonnia.*

UN FLAMBEAU, JEANNETTE, ISABELLE, page 128, comes from Provence. Nicholas Saboly (1614–1675) is often given credit for composing it as well as a number of other Provençal carols. If not the composer, he was an excellent compiler, and deserves commendation for getting some very fine carols down on paper. The translation of the seventeenth century text is by E. Cuthbert Nunn (1868–1914), a British organist and composer.

The manger, or *crèche,* is the center of Christmas festivities in France. Both at home and in the church, ceremonies are conducted around it. The verses of this carol lend themselves well to being acted out beside the manger.

Torchlight processions on Christmas Eve are also a French tradition. Children dressed as shepherds carry torches or candles as they go to church for midnight Mass. Sometimes, drums and fifes or tuned whistles are included in the cortège, and *Pat-a-Pan* (page 112) joins *Un Flambeau, Jeannette, Isabelle* as a musical accompaniment for the paraders.

VENI, EMMANUEL, page 312, is a Gregorian theme based on the seven antiphons performed at Vespers during the Christmas season. Each verse addresses Christ with titles given him in the Scriptures.

The melody is a combination of several *Kyrie* tunes assembled by Thomas Helmore from a French Missal he found in the National Library of Portugal in 1854.

A VIRGIN UNSPOTTED, page 42. One of the most cheerful of the early Ballad Carols, it appeared in print as early as 1734. Many different tunes have been used with the text. One of the favorites was included in Davies Gilbert's *Some Ancient Christmas Carols,* dated 1822. The version given here appeared in Sandys (1833). An alternate title, *A Virgin Most Pure,* is often used for this carol.

VOM HIMMEL HOCH, DA KOMM'ICH HER, page 161. Martin Luther's verses for this carol, written in 1535, were based on an older folk song, *Aus Fremden Landen Komm Ich Her.* In 1539, he set the text to the fine tune used here. We are uncertain whether he composed it himself or borrowed it. Luther wrote the song for his children, and the original was a 15-verse dialogue between an angel and the shepherds. In our version, the first two verses belong to the angel, the last to the shepherds.

Luther was an ardent music lover and a champion of its use in the church. He wrote in 1524: "I am willing to write German psalms following the example of the prophets and ancient fathers." Another time, he said, "I truly desire that all Christians love and regard as worthy the lovely gift of music, which is a precious, acceptable, and costly treasure given to mankind by God."

WASSAIL SONG, page 35. This begging carol hies from Yorkshire. Broadsides dated as early as 1829 have included its text.

WE THREE KINGS OF ORIENT ARE, page 66, is one of the few American carols to achieve an international reputation. It is very popular in England, and was the only American carol included in the collection, *Christmas Carols, New and Old,* by Bramley and Stainer.

The mixture of major and minor modes gives this carol an archaic flavor, and it has often been mistaken for being much older than it really is. Dr. John H. Hopkins wrote both the words and music around 1857 while serving as Rector of Christ Church in Williamsport, Pennsylvania.

WHAT CHILD IS THIS? page 30. The tune, *Greensleeves,* is a love song from Elizabethan times. Shakespeare used it several times in his plays.

Sir John Stainer (1840–1901) who made the harmonization given here, is responsible for arrangements of many carols that have become standard versions. A distinguished composer and organist, Stainer began his musical training as a chorister at Saint Paul's Cathedral in London when he was seven years old. Eventually, he became organist of Saint Paul's, serving from 1847 to 1856, when failing eyesight forced him to resign. He also was organist at Oxford and received both a Bachelor and Doctor of Music from the University. Queen Victoria knighted him in 1888.

William Dix, author of the words, earned his living as the manager of a marine insurance company in Bristol. In his spare time, he wrote many fine hymns of lasting value.

WHILE SHEPHERDS WATCHED THEIR FLOCKS, page 31. Nahum Tate, poet laureate of England at the time, wrote this hymn as a literal verse transcription of chapter 2 of *The Gospel According to Saint Luke,* verses 8–15.

The hymn is sung to several different tunes. The one chosen here is an adaptation of a soprano aria from a lesser-known opera by Handel, *Siroë, King of Persia.*

WIE SCHÖN LEUCHTET DER MORGENSTERN, page 164, was written by Philipp Nicolai during the disastrous plague of 1597 in which over a thousand members of his parish died. In the midst of the sorrow and distress of the pestilence, Nicolai was seized by a religious ecstasy during which he wrote both the words and music of this chorale in about three hours. It stands today as one of the great monuments of German hymnody.

W ZLOBIE LEZY, page 204. The Polish name for carols is *Kolendy.* This is a very old composition, probably originating in the thirteenth or fourteenth century.

GUITAR CHORDS

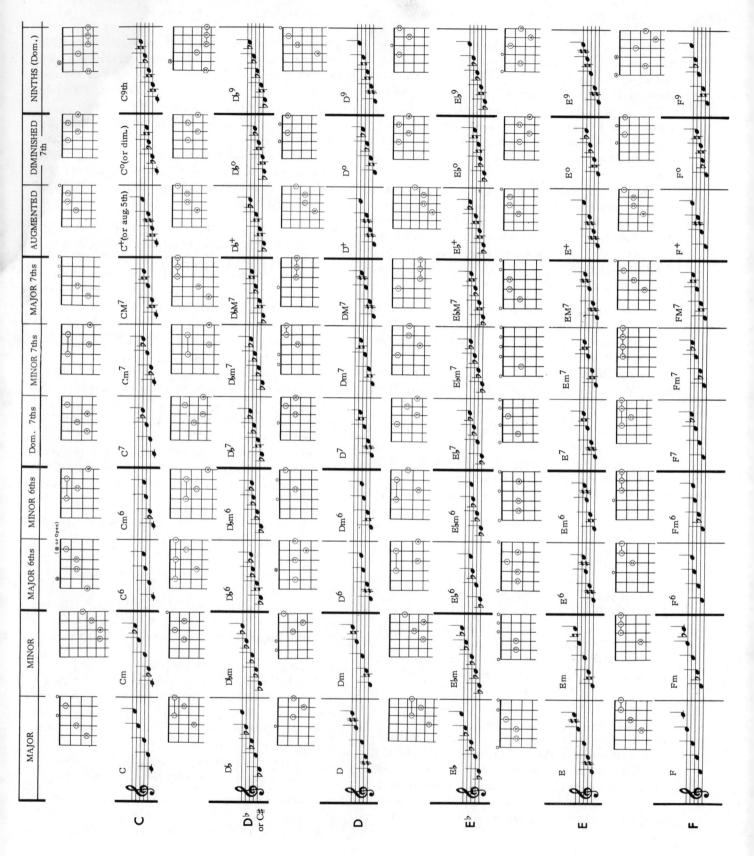

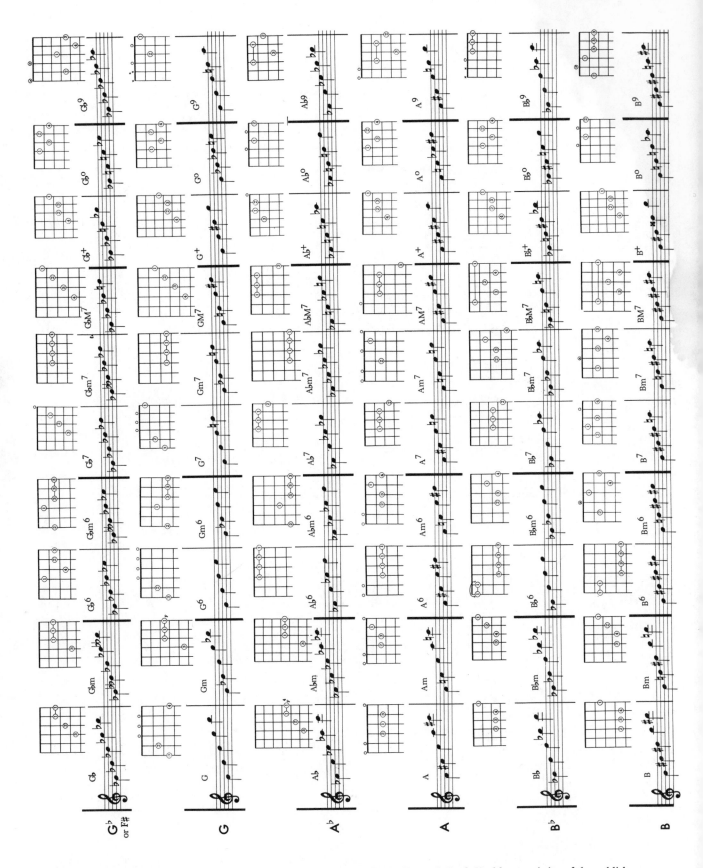

Adapted from *Tennessee Ernie Ford's Book of Favorite Hymns*, © 1962 by Ernest J. Ford. Used by permission of the publishers, Prentice-Hall, Inc.

INDEX OF TITLES

The country of origin of each carol is indicated by the symbol on the left: A=Austria; CA=Canada; CH=Chile; CO=Columbia; CZ=Czechoslovakia; D=Denmark; E=England; F=France; G=Germany; H=Hungary; I=Italy; M=Mexico; NE=The Netherlands; NO=Norway; P=Poland; PR=Puerto Rico; R=Roumania; S=Spain; SC=Scotland; SW=Sweden; US=United States; V=Venezuela; W=Wales.

337